BUILDING CULTURE

A HANDBOOK TO HARNESSING HUMAN NATURE
TO CREATE STRONG SCHOOL TEAMS

LEKHA SHARMA

DESIGNED BY OLIVER CAVIGLIOLI

First published 2023

by John Catt Educational Ltd,
15 Riduna Park, Station Road,
Melton, Woodbridge IP12 1QT

Tel: +44 (0) 1394 389850
Email: enquiries@johncatt.com
Website: www.johncatt.com

Opinions expressed in this publication are those
of the contributors and are not necessarily those
of the publishers or the editors. We cannot accept
responsibility for any errors or omissions.

ISBN: 978 1 915 261 41 0

Typeset by John Catt Educational Limited

For my grandmother, my mother, my mother-in-law, and my sister – three generations of women who have consistently modelled courage, determination and strength, and taught me just how important it is to be 'fearless in the pursuit of what sets our soul on fire'. I hope to pass these learnings onto my darling daughter Ava, shine bright little one!

Reviews

Kate Jones,
Senior Associate
for Teaching and
Learning with
Evidence Based
Education

Knowledge is power. Culture is key. This wonderful book by Lekha Sharma offers school leaders knowledge and guidance, from experience and evidence, to build a culture in schools for everyone to thrive. From psychological safety to trust, flexibility and wisdom, this book captures key messages that are essential to supporting wellbeing and empowering staff. Interesting, insightful and informative. A recommended read for all school leaders and aspiring leaders.

Nicole McCartney,
Director of
Education,
Creative Education
Trust

Lekha does a wonderful job of straddling theory and practical example to show that gone are the days of the saviour or the cape. Effective leadership is instead clearing the path, ensuring your teams know what is at the end of that path, what part they play in the journey and that you will give them everything they need to be successful when you reach the destination together.

Tom Bennett, Lead
Behaviour Adviser
for Schools to
the Department
of Education,
Founder of
ResearchED

An extremely good and long-awaited book that finally addresses whole-school issues at the right level and through the right lens. How can something as complex as an institution be run with any kind of success without this vital framework? Lekha Sharma has written a readable, evidence-informed discussion of the subject that is both accessible and rooted in research *and* practice which makes it an important read for anyone whose business is raising the bar for student and staff standards in a sustainable and meaningful way. I commend this to you.

Peps Mccrea,
Dean at Ambition
Institute, Director
at Steplab

Beautifully written, tons of fresh thinking, eminently practical, and stunningly put together – seriously, what more could teachers and leaders ask for in an edubook?

Acknowledgements

Mark Twain

'There is no such thing as a new idea. It is impossible. We simply take a lot of old ideas and put them into a sort of mental kaleidoscope. We give them a turn and they make new and curious combinations. We keep on turning and making new combinations indefinitely; but they are the same old pieces of coloured glass that have been in use through all the ages.'

Thank you to all the wonderful colleagues that have contributed their wisdom, supported my thinking (and rethinking), and have generously given their time to support the book. A few special thank-yous to the wonderful bunch below.

OLIVER CAVIGLIOLI

NIMISH LAD

JADE PEARCE

HEENA DAVE

KATE STOCKINGS

PEPS MCCREA

SAM CROME

YAMINA BIBI

MARY MYATT

JAMIE SCOTT

KATIE WALTON

KARREN KNOWLTON

ALISON PEACOCK

Contents

CHAPTERS

1	2	3	4	5	6	7	8	9
PAGE 15	PAGE 31	PAGE 45	PAGE 59	PAGE 69	PAGE 83	PAGE 95	PAGE 105	

INTRODUCTION

Introduction

Setting the scene.

Knowledge is power. As school leaders, despite the dirty connotations that come with the word, we all aspire to having the kind of power that effects positive change in our schools. In 2022, 59% of pupils met the expected standard in reading, writing and mathematics. Post-pandemic impact aside, this means that in 2022, 41% of pupils nationally were not academically prepared for the next stage of their education. Now more than ever, school leaders need to be equipped with the knowledge, skill and, most importantly, support to drive standards up and make strides in recovering from the COVID-19 pandemic. High expectations must be met with high levels of support.

➕
There are four leadership NPQs and four teaching NPQs.

We're in an exciting age of professional development for leaders with reforms meaning that a suite of National Professional Qualifications is available for leaders at all levels to support their leadership journey. Despite this access to knowledge-rich professional learning, leaders are still very much up against it on multiple fronts. In a survey conducted by Teacher Tapp (Greany et al, 2022), two out of five leaders (42%) said they had been 'mostly surviving' when asked about their experiences of working in school since the start of the pandemic. Leaders are not only dealing with the academic fall-out of the pandemic but also have the task of supporting their staff with the emotional fall-out that the pandemic has left behind (UCL News, 2022).

➕
UCL News (2022): 35% of 18-29s said that they felt in control of their mental health, compared to 47% of 30-59s and 61% of older adults.

As we navigate this complex educational landscape, what has become clear is that leaders not only need knowledge of the *what* of curriculum, assessment, pedagogy, and a host of other domains but also need knowledge of the *how*. How can school leaders bring together the theoretical knowledge they possess and mobilise it on the ground so that they can have a positive and tangible impact on pupil outcomes? Teachers are increasingly equipped with the awareness and knowledge of cognitive psychology but what other areas of psychology could support those that lead those very teachers? And what elements of human nature can we harness in order to build the kind of school cultures that are conducive to improving outcomes for pupils?

This book isn't an in-depth analysis of culture and how to get it right but it does highlight some key aspects of cultivating the kind of culture that leads to great pupil outcomes, rooted both in my own experiences as a senior leader on the ground and from the report by the Evidence Based Education (2022) 'School Environment and Leadership: Evidence Review'. My aim in writing this is to urge leaders to consider the far-reaching impact they have on those they lead and to consider *how* they do things, not just *what* they do. Ultimately, systems and knowledge are crucial but, mobilised by wallies in weak school cultures, they simply aren't enough for us to make sufficient gains for the pupils we serve. I don't claim to know how to get leadership and culture 'right' and I openly recognise that as humans we are all flawed, but I do strongly believe that without exploring this territory we leave stones unturned and any stone unturned in the pursuit of improving outcomes for pupils is always worth exploring.

This isn't about 'gaming' leadership and isn't intended to be interpreted as a collection of manipulation tactics to be employed blindly by leaders. Rather, I hope this acts as a tool to prompt careful consideration of implementation in schools. It offers just one perspective that, despite being distilled into chapters, is fraught with complexity and nuance. I, therefore, attempt to offer counterpoints and challenges as well as further notes in the margin of the book. Physicists call this reference-frame dependent: the ability to accept the complexity of something and examine it from different perspectives.

And if even one leader reflects on their practices and rethinks how they are behaving, interacting or 'doing something', I'll consider the job done.

Educational leadership – what is it anyway?

What is leadership? How do we define leadership? Is educational leadership different to leadership in other fields? How do we equip leaders with the knowledge and attributes they need to lead their teams well? These are just some of the questions that have been posed and debated in the world of education for many years and educators continue to do so. It is not my aim, nor within my reach, to 'solve' the problem of educational leadership in this book. Instead I aim to offer some important human components of school culture that school leaders may benefit from having an awareness of. To set the scene more broadly, I would like to draw upon the work of David M Gurr from his paper entitled 'Educational Leadership Research: Is there a compelling reason to change?' Gurr synthesises his research in the field of education and educational leadership over the course of 55 years. He opens by sharing the nature of his research and his use of multiple, perspective, observational case studies to uncover whether current research questions around leadership are worthwhile, in response to the earlier work of Scott Eacott. Gurr points to the consensus around four key areas of common practice amongst school leaders:

1 | Articulating a vision

2 | Helping people develop and are people-centred

3 | Leading change

4 | Improving teaching and learning

He goes on to assert that there is no formula for 'effective school leadership' but rather these leaders take from several views of leadership to create their own personal leadership approach, bespoke to their context and circumstances. 'They become a sense maker to help others understand a school's place in a complex set of contexts.'

Gurr's statement about educational leadership, rooted in his own and other researchers' findings, highlights a key point about 'the nature of leadership'. All the four areas of common practice require a human component; the ability for leaders to influence and change behaviour to achieve an end goal. The reason I cite Gurr is because he adopts a personal narrative approach in making the above statement about leadership. This, in my eyes, is the best way to tackle the messy business of educational leadership. The social dynamics inherent in the work that leaders do day-in, day-out demand a socially considered approach.

Arguments have been made that this side of educational leadership is difficult to quantify and codify and, in some cases, these considerations have been disregarded or sidelined.[1] However, we can all agree that educational leadership (whatever this may be!) is a person-centred and humanistic endeavour. The focus of this book is not in addressing this debate but rather offering a contribution of how leaders can deepen their understand of how humans operate and therefore how to best lead their teams.

Educational policy may change. Educational discourse may change. But one enduring fact is this – we are all human and will continue to be human.

References

Department for Education. (2022). *National professional qualifications (NPQs)* [online]. bit.ly/3TuLlMz.

Evidence Based Education (2022). 'School Environment and Leadership: Evidence Review', [online]. bit.ly/3XLG45f

Greany, T., Thomson, P., Cousin, S., Martindale, N., University of Nottingham, University of Oxford, in partnership with NAHT and ASCL. (Spring 2022). Leading after Lockdown: Research on school leaders' work, well-being and career intentions (Phase 2 findings) [online]. bit.ly/3CwUVHC.

Gurr, D. M. (2019). Educational Leadership Research: Is there a compelling reason to change?, *Research in Educational Administration and Leadership*, 4 (1), 148-164.

UCL News. (2022). 'Worries about finances outstrip concerns about catching Covid-19', University City London [online]. bit.ly/3TarEJW.

1
This argument is not without merit; if we cannot codify these 'human' elements of leadership clearly then how can we possibly integrate these into any formal form of leadership development? An awareness of these concepts, however, may be a reasonable starting point.

| | **A culture of** |
| Chapter 1 | **psychological safety** |

CHAPTERS

| 1 | 2 | 3 | 4 | 5 | 6 | 7 | 8 | 15 |
| PAGE 15 | PAGE 31 | PAGE 45 | PAGE 59 | PAGE 69 | PAGE 83 | PAGE 95 | PAGE 105 | |

CHAPTER 1

A CULTURE OF PSYCHOLOGICAL SAFETY

A culture of psychological safety

Psychological safety can cause breakthroughs in performance.

Psychological safety enables everyone to feel seen and heard without the fear of repercussions. It creates conditions where nothing is 'off the table' and honest conversations are had about the (actual!) state of play and how we can strengthen our professional practice. Psychological safety coupled with high expectations results in the potential for better performance.

The idea of psychological safety stems from a branch of psychology known as 'organisational psychology'. This is a clear example of how the broader field has much more to offer beyond cognitive psychology, especially in guiding school leaders in how to affect positive change in their schools.

The idea of psychological safety was first established in the 1960s but interest in the idea waned and later resurfaced in the 1990s when organisational psychologist William Kahn published his paper 'Psychological Conditions of Personal Engagement and Disengagement at Work'. In this paper, Kahn defined three conditions that were necessary for personal engagement at work:

1 | Psychological availability: the psychological resources required to invest in one's role.

2 | Psychological meaningfulness: the sense of return on these 'investments'.

3 | Psychological safety: the sense of being able to show oneself without fear of negative repercussions.[1]

Amy Edmondson, a professor at Harvard Business School, continued exploration of this concept and defines psychological safety as 'a belief that one will not be punished or humiliated for speaking up with ideas, questions, concerns or mistakes' and that the team is safe for interpersonal risk-taking or 'permission for candour'.

1
This argument is not without merit; if we cannot codify these 'human' elements of leadership clearly, then how can we possibly integrate these into any formal form of leadership development? An awareness of these concepts, however, may be a reasonable starting point.

As part of her research, Edmondson joined a team of physicians and nurses at a hospital to explore the rates of human-related drug errors – that is, the number of times the incorrect dose of a medicine or the incorrect medicine altogether was administered in several hospitals. She had a simple question to answer: 'Do better teams make fewer errors?' Edmondson collected data on the drug errors over a period of six months and the results were entirely unexpected. The data the team collected showed that better teams made more not fewer mistakes. Edmondson, upon processing this rather puzzling data, decided to send a research assistant to the eight hospital units to see if he could find out more about what was leading to the stark differences in data. He found that the distinguishing factor in units that had higher numbers of errors was their ability and willingness to talk about the errors themselves. She later termed this climate of 'openness' as psychological safety.

In Edmondson's research, psychological safety led to more errors. How is that possibly a good thing? What Edmondson concluded was that when people were able to discuss their errors more openly, the frequency of these errors that occurred would reduce in the long-term. This also enabled these teams to work together collaboratively to find innovative ways to address and avoid these errors in the future.

As detailed in Edmondson and Lei's 2014 paper 'Psychological Safety: The History, Renaissance, and Future of an Interpersonal Construct', they state that 'extensive research suggests that psychological safety enables teams and organizations to learn'.

Let's dig deeper into how this concept may be applied to that of school improvement by school leaders…

Dr Neil Gilbride, senior lecturer at the University of Gloucestershire, refers to the work of Hawkins and James (2017) in describing how schools are complex organisations.

A culture of psychological safety

Neil Gilbride

Cambridge
Assessment
Network and
Research Blog
2022

'Hawkins and James describe many schools' features in their seminal paper, characterizing them as C. E. L. L. S – Complex, Evolving, Loosely Linked Systems. Complex can mean, among other features, that each part of a school system is deeply interconnected. Consequently, one part of a system can interacts in many different direct and indirect ways with its other parts. These interactions are crucial because through them completely new variables can emerge. This means systems can move between stability and change and become very difficult to describe. After all, how do you describe something which is so deeply interconnected, interacting, and with the capacity for change?'

In such a complex environment, errors are not only likely but inevitable. This begs the question: is it better to be making errors that have a direct impact on pupil achievement and hiding them or is it better to be quickly identifying them and dealing with them before they impact pupil achievement at all? The answer is a no-brainer and it is my argument that psychological safety within schools becomes imperative in ensuring that the latter is achieved.

Huang et al (2008) put forth a model in which psychological safety leads to team performance through group learning. Their research studying members of 60 research and development teams in Taiwain supports the idea that being able to speak openly through dialogue, decision making, and discussion is a determinant of high group performance. This highlights another valuable component of cultivating psychological safety within our schools – laying the foundations for strong professional learning communities.

Stoll, Bolam,
McMahon,
Thomas, Wallace,
Greenwood and
Hawkey, 2006

'A professional learning community is an inclusive group of people, motivated by a shared learning vision, who support and work with each other, finding ways, inside and outside their immediate community, to enquire on their practice and together learn new and better approaches that will enhance all pupils' learning.'

Excellent teaching is a constant education.

If excellent teaching means excellent pupil outcomes (and subsequent life outcomes) then this should be every school's sole goal. In a world of lesson gradings and 'outstanding teacher' badges, complacency and diminishing standards are inevitable. However, in a world where a climate of genuine psychological safety means that teachers are able to accept and act upon feedback and coaching, in their relentless drive to hone their craft, teaching practice will no doubt improve. I intentionally reference the word 'genuine' because faux psychological safety is absolutely a thing and leads to 'cordial hypocrisy' where people pretend there is trust when in fact there is none. Psychological safety is not a shiny cloak to be donned proudly by school leaders but rather needs to be woven into every thread of school life and must be less about the leader asserting a sense of their own righteousness and more about providing staff with the conditions to thrive as professionals.

Psychological safety also plays another important role within schools – teacher wellbeing. Teacher wellbeing has deservedly become a point of emphasis for school leaders in more recent years and although more superficial measures such as yoga classes and croissants in the staff room are employed and often warmly welcomed, they do not offer a lasting or sustainable solution to the issue. This can be found in not only the systems and structures that offer a consistent and predictable drumbeat to school life but to the culture of the school. A positive school culture can be exemplified in many ways, but psychological safety and openness is undoubtedly a marker, enabling all members of staff within a school to feel comfortable and safe in airing their opinions, ideas, thoughts and feelings about their work and the organisation. In the absence of this, a culture of distrust and wariness is created leaving people feeling constantly on edge and unsurprisingly not on their best form.

Teaching is a person-centred profession. Taking the humanity out of our leadership serves no one, least the pupils.

Evidence based education-teacher wellbeing

In Robert Coe's 2022 paper 'School Environment and Leadership: Evidence Review', he aims to outline the features of school environment and leadership practices that make a difference to pupil learning, having summarised the current evidence and literature on school leadership. One of the potential indicators identified conducive to growth in pupil attainment is 'teacher wellbeing' and the associated outcomes of 'job satisfaction, morale, organisational commitment and stress management'. Coe defines teacher wellbeing as 'the extent to which teachers are happy and fulfilled in their work', including aspects such as:

- Job satisfaction
- Morale
- Happiness
- Organisational commitment
- Intention to remain at the school
- Perception of workload, stress, work/life balance
- Occupational self-regulation (the ability to balance commitment to work with distance from work)

Coe cites the work of Ladd (2011) and Sims & Jerrim (2020) who concluded that wellbeing predicts teachers' intentions to leave a school. This – considering the evidence that teacher turnover negatively impacts student outcomes – begins to paint a picture of why actively retaining teachers within schools and carefully considering the school's professional 'offer' are indeed significant. As curriculum leaders, we have a subject offer. As inclusion leaders, we have an inclusion offer. But what is our professional offer to those teachers within our organisations? What commitments do we make to ensure that they flourish? I share this idea tentatively, knowing that it could be misconstrued as a marketing/recruitment strategy. However, by defining and verbalising our commitment, we are more likely to abide by it. It is, therefore, within this 'offer' that psychological safety could be considered. Coe defines leadership trust as encompassing feelings of 'psychological safety', it being ok to take a risk or make a mistake. Psychological safety, as a component of leadership trust, highlights an important and closely linked core concept – that of trust.

Trust is crucial

Coe (2022) points to clear definition and conceptualisation of trust offered by Tschannen-Moran & Hoy (2000): the 'willingness to be vulnerable to another party based on the confidence that the latter party is a) benevolent b) reliable c) competent d) honest and e) open'. These factors of trust illuminate the multi-faceted nature of the construct and further highlights how complex the notion and enactment of psychological safety can be. In the domain-specific context of schools, Coe (2022) outlines that leadership trust is 'the belief that leaders are well-intentioned, competent, honest, caring, forgiving and consistent' and that 'teachers have a willingness to share or expose vulnerabilities'. What this looks like on the ground is further explored in the final section of this chapter.

Trust, in and of itself, has been explored as a focus for interdisciplinary research for decades. Despite this, the literature around it has been inconsistent and the origins of the concept unclear. In their book *Building Trust*, Robert Solomon and Fernando Flores succinctly summarise what I feel is the challenge with equipping leaders purely with knowledge and no more: 'Building trust begins with an honest understanding of trust but it also requires everyday routines and practices. Without the practices, that understanding comes to nothing.' We will delve deeper into the idea of trust in chapter 3.

The following case study comes from Sam Crome who will share the everyday practices and routines he has applied to his team on the ground to support the development of trust and subsequent psychological safety.

Case study: Cultivating psychological safety

I have been researching both psychological safety and high-performance teaming for the last two years, and then trying out various findings on some of the teams I lead. One conclusion I quickly reached was that Amy

Sam Crome

Edmondson's work on psychological safety is integral to the success of teams. Almost every evidence-informed aspect of successful teamwork does not work without a foundation of psychological safety in a team. It underpins everything. Here are some ways that I try to apply psychological safety principles to my leadership:

Take regular temperature checks

There are different surveys you can use that aim to assess a team's psychological safety. They can be fascinating, illuminating, and slightly daunting for team leaders. I recently worked with a large team of managers from a well-known social media platform to help them understand how psychologically safe the team was. Prior to the work that I did, we sent out a psychological safety survey. The results were interesting. While members agreed that the team was supportive and that colleagues were friendly and collegiate, they were less favourable regarding the team's culture of sharing ideas and owning mistakes. It turned out that the team's leaders had never really created a narrative or culture where bad news was shared or less successful projects were reflected on or framed as learning experiences. The result was a group that weren't sure if their views or ideas would be welcomed for fear that they might be 'wrong'. I would recommend using a survey (see psychsafety.co.uk) to understand your starting point in the team – taking the temperature is the only way that you'll know how the team can improve.

Invite feedback and model the process

As a leader, it's easier to present an idea or initative, explain it to the team, and roll it out, than it is to invite critique and feedback at all stages. Feedback can be hard to hear. It takes time. It can mean sacrificing hours of previous work to move in another direction. But if we are to get the most out of our teams, both in terms of their motivation, commitment, and expertise, we need to ask for feedback.

This should be normalised in the team's culture. For example, in team meetings a leader should ask for feedback, either about a project that the team has been working on, or their own contributions to the team. The key to psychological safety is the team feeling just that – safe to try things, safe to give feedback, safe to receive feedback. As a leader, it's our role to model that process to the group – both asking for feedback and how we respond to it.

Another method is to use surveys to see how the team feels about something before a meeting, and then using the in-person time to discuss the results and to own the feedback you received. Frame the feedback positively so the team can see how it will benefit you, and their work, in the future.

Once giving and receiving feedback has been modelled by the leader, someone who thinks like a scientist in the pursuit of finding out objective truths, it becomes normalised for the team to do that with each other.

Admit your mistakes and ask for help

Many teams hide their mistakes, both on an individual and group level. Successes are celebrated; mistakes are ignored or even receive blame. Owen Eastwood talks about sharing the pain in his book *Belonging*. He comments that tribal communities would quite literally carve their mistakes on the walls, a memorable and lasting chance to learn from something that went wrong. Once you frame mistakes or failures as learning opportunities, or to quote Amy Edmondson 'decouple fear and failure', the team can start to utilise every team action as a chance to improve.

I find it useful as a leader to own it when things don't go perfectly. That usually involves discussing with a team what we aimed to do, what happened, and what things went wrong along the way. Or which things I didn't get right personally, that I am keen to learn from.

Practically, I think it's worth building in time for meetings or debriefs where you 'share the pain' or, for want of a better term, 'how we can learn from our

A culture of psychological safety

recent experiences'. This is how I would manage that discussion: firstly, pose the questions – what can we learn from? What could have gone better? The team can then discuss in smaller subgroups of two or four about this before feeding back to the wider team. The leader can find trends, positively frame what has been said, and celebrate the mistakes as the learning opportunities that they are.

Importantly, these moments can be narrated and recalled further down the line once something has improved or been addressed. The team will be galvanised when they see the fruits of these discussions, discussions that can be tricky to feel confident about at first. Part of admitting mistakes is the team, and its leader, feeling comfortable about asking for help. It's the leader's role to regularly draw upon the expertise among the group, acknowledging their own shortfall in an area before asking someone else to assist them. We can't expect teams to share their mistakes and ask for help, if the leader has overseen a culture of know-it-all-ism, or individuals working as silos to enhance their own reputations.

Build a learning culture

Dan Cable suggests that everyone has a seeking system, a desire to learn and develop. We can activate our team's seeking system by building a learning culture. In my experience, psychologically safe teams are ones that learn together and grow. Psychological safety, as we know, is about creating the right environment for people to be themselves and have a voice; when you surround yourself with others who are activating their own seeking system, another layer of team cohesion and trust is built.

So, what does this look like practically?

One method I have used with pastoral leaders is to put team learning at the heart of every meeting. In our first year working together, I would give out a chapter from a book, or an article/blog post, and the team had two weeks to read it and think about it before the following meeting. Then, that meeting would begin with a discussion on the reading materials, covering what we liked, what we found interesting, and if or how we could apply these ideas to our roles as school leaders. The following year, we bought team members a book of their choice, so long as it was from genres such as leadership, education, high performance, etc. Each team member was on a rota, fulfilling the same duty that I had done the previous year. Every meeting must start with this sort of shared learning – it's a powerful way to begin and makes it clear to everyone that before anything else, we learn and grow as a group.

The team move from the learning section of a meeting into more operational discussions with a sense of purpose and satisfaction, but more than that, a sense of unity that we just did something great together. That, I have found, is a superb catalyst for honest, open discussions and a group of people finding joint solutions to problems.

Normalise and embrace conflict

Beware quiet, compliant team interactions and meetings. Psychologically safe teams engage with each other's ideas, and this inevitably leads to conflict. It's worth us reframing the word, because conflict doesn't need to create relational issues between team members – conflict is simply about the team experiencing different ideas or not immediately agreeing on a course of action.

It helps if the team has an existing, agreed narrative of how conflict helps the team improve. We will disagree on things, we will work together to iron out differences of opinion, and ultimately, we will use our collective diversity as a strength. It's important that when we disagree, we remember that it is not personal, that we are a team, and that we are working together for the best possible outcome.

The team could use a framework to help them understand how to navigate giving and receiving feedback so that the conflict that arises is handled constructively and positively. *Radical Candor: How to Get What You Want* by Kim Scott is an excellent example of a book that helps the reader understand both why being candid in important, but also how to manage situations where difficult feedback or conflict is required.

Essentially the team needs to see that task-related conflict that focuses on processes or team decisions (and avoids relationship/personal conflict) can be a healthy driver for open communication, team effectiveness, and psychological safety.

Psychological safety takes time

Sam's case study offers invaluable insight into how psychological safety can be cultivated on the ground and what practical approaches can be adopted in trying to build this element of culture. However, the complexity of school leadership and school improvement means this is no easy feat. So, what are the pitfalls when it comes to psychological safety? Here I'll explore the barriers involved in creating psychologically safe cultures, to avoid a reductionist and simplistic take on what is a frankly messy business.

Psychological safety, like school culture, takes time. A leader I once worked with told me that culture was geology. At the time, the impatient school leader in me didn't quite understand this but looking back now it is a useful analogy to illuminate the point. The openness and ability to admit our mistakes to another doesn't evolve over night. No matter how trustworthy or wonderful a leader you may be in your first few weeks in post, we cannot expect people to trust blindly. Nor can we expect trust to be sustained, without work, over time.

Solomon and
Flores, 2001

'Although trust seems invisible (transparent and simply taken for granted), it is the result of continuous attentiveness and activity. Trust, once established, easily recedes into the background, into a familiar and therefore barely conscious set of habits and practices... Trust often becomes visible (introspect) only when it has been challenged or violated.'

This presents a clear challenge of developing psychological safety: sustaining it. After all, we're all flawed beings and we're all prone to, in the spirit of psychological safety, getting it epically wrong! So, what happens when we create conditions for psychological safety but it's damaged through natural human error on the leader's part? As we all know, word spreads quickly within organisations. Soon, one small human error can challenge people's perceptions and beliefs about a leader at an organisational level. The beauty of mitigating against this challenge? It loops back to the construct of psychological safety and feeling safe enough to admit our errors and mistakes, in the knowledge that others will accept these for what they are – errors – just as you do as a leader. I recognise the simplicity and potential reductionist take on this but in a culture where it's ok for people to make mistakes and learn from them, it's ok for *everyone* at *every level* to make mistakes and learn from them. Professional learning communities aren't just for novices but for all.

This is just one of many considerations when it comes to the challenges associated with this component of school culture and that's not to say there's more. By acknowledging and recognising these and having a 'cards on the table' approach we allow ourselves as leaders to extract the value that *is* there, rather than critique the value that may not be.

Summary

Feeling safe enough within your school team to make mistakes, openly talk about them, or even to say 'I don't know' without fear of judgement or backlash affects your performance. If we want to get our school culture right, we must consider how psychologically safe our school environments are and actively try to cultivate this on an ongoing basis.

Reflective questions for your school

1. How psychologically safe is the school culture at present?

2. What might I do differently in the short/medium/long term that might impact how psychologically safe it feels?

3. What are the barriers of a psychologically safe culture? How could these be mitigated against practically?

References

Bolam, R., McMahon, A., Stoll, L., Thomas, S., Wallace, M., Greenwood, A., Hawkey, K. and Smith, M. (2005). *Creating and sustaining effective professional learning communities.* London: Department for Education and Skills.

Coe, R. (2022). 'School Environment and Leadership: Evidence Review', Evidence Based Education. Available at: bit.ly/3ZUM7q5.

Edmondson, A. (1999). Psychological safety and learning behavior in work teams. *Administrative Science Quarterly*, 44 (2), 350-383.

Edmondson, A and Lei, Z. (2014). Psychological safety: The history, renaissance, and future of an interpersonal construct. *Annual Review of Organizational Psychology and Organizational Behavior*, 1, 23-43.

Gilbride, D. (2022). [online] Cambridgeassessment.org.uk. Available at: cambridgeassessment.org.uk/blogs/complexity-wicked-problems/

Hawkins, M. and James, C. (2017). 'Developing a perspective on schools as complex, evolving, loosely linking systems'. *Educational Management Administration & Leadership*, 46 (5), 729-748.

Huang, C. C., Chu, C. Y. and Jiang, P. C. (2008). An Empirical Study of Psychological Safety and Performance in Technology R&D Teams.

Kahn, W. A. (1990). Psychological conditions of personal engagement and disengagement at work. *Academy of Management Journal*, 33, 692-724.

Ladd, H. F. (2011). Teachers' perceptions of their working conditions. *Educational Evaluation and Policy Analysis*, 33 (2), 235-261.

Sims, S. and Jerrim, J. (2020). TALIS 2018: Teacher working conditions, turnover and attrition. Available at: files.eric.ed.gov/fulltext/ED604489.pdf.

Solomon, R. C. and Flores, F. (2001). *Building trust in business, politics, relationships, and life.* New York: Oxford University Press.

Tschannen-Moran, M. and Hoy, W. K. (2000). A multidisciplinary analysis of the nature, meaning, and measurement of trust. Review of Educational Research, 70 (4), 547-593.

CHAPTERS

1
PAGE 15

2
PAGE 31

3
PAGE 45

4
PAGE 59

5
PAGE 69

6
PAGE 83

7
PAGE 95

8
PAGE 105

29

Chapter 2 | A culture of purpose

CHAPTER 2

A CULTURE OF PURPOSE

A clear sense of purpose can anchor school improvement efforts.

Houman Hourani,
Harvard Graduate
School of
Education

'It's usually registered as whining… *why do we have to do this?* But it's a good question.'

Having absolute clarity about our collective purpose in schools means that every single person within a school community is moving in the same direction. If I know why I'm doing something, I'm more likely to do it. During times of uncertainty, change and challenge, our purpose is the sturdy anchor that keeps us grounded.

What is our purpose? What do we stand for? Why do we do what we do? These are all examples of how purpose is explored in organisations and in schools. Often, these questions make an appearance in September inset days or inspirational speeches from senior members of staff, but they are so much more than this. Purpose, both establishing and sustaining it, deserves far more attention when it comes to strong school cultures and should be more than just tokenistic sentiments sporadically espoused.

In an independent review titled 'Creating a Culture: How school leaders can optimise behaviour' (2017), Tom Bennett explores commonly found features of excellent school culture. Bennett defines culture 'as the way we do things around here', a concept dating back to the '90s from the work of organisational consultant and thought leader Warren Bennis. Bennett offers a breakdown of the different components of strong school culture that they found in their independent review of behaviour in schools. Although the report refers to school culture, specifically in the context of driving behaviour in schools, I argue that elements that Bennett highlights offer invaluable support for leaders in driving school culture more widely.

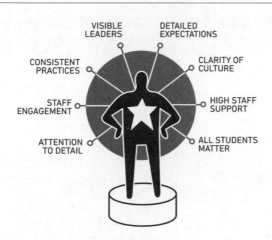

Figure 1: Creating a culture

Feature of excellent school culture	What might it look like in practice?
Visible leaders	• Leaders on gates in the morning and at the end of day • Leaders walking the corridors and regular interaction with pupils/teachers alike • Leaders out on the playground • Leaders running towards not away from 'trouble'
Detailed expectations	• Clarity over what's expected • Clarity on 'what good looks like', e.g. exemplification • Shared examples of best practice • Repetition of the expectation and the purpose it serves
Clarity of culture	• Making clear 'how things are done around here' • Positive reinforcement of acts that embody the culture • Transparency when culture is not enacted • Walking the talk

Feature of excellent school culture	What might it look like in practice?
High staff support	• Prioritising professional learning • Offering bespoke support for teachers at different stages of their career • Offering a sequence of professional learning to embed practice • Staff voice surveys on what professional support they require/want
All students matter	• An inclusive approach that considers the needs of all pupils • High expectations of all pupils regardless of their starting points • Pupil progress meetings that focus on the child not just the data
Attention to detail	• Following up on professional learning to ensure practices are embedded as intended • Regular but kind quality assurance to ensure policies and ways of doing things are being enacted accurately
Staff engagement	• Staff voice regularly surveyed • An open door culture where all staff feel like they can air their thoughts, ideas and feelings • A collaborative approach, where possible, to decision making (at every level)
Consistent practices	• Codifying common practice as a reference point for all staff • Signposting examples of best practice to exemplify practices • Coaching staff to support them with their professional development

In this chapter, I focus closely on two features as identified above: clarity of culture and consistent practices, how this influences school-wide culture and how it can be achieved. I also explore how this culture, or 'how we do things around here', is reinforced by social norms. Having a clear purpose and a clear reason for why we do things the way we do is an integral part of school culture. If you have spent time at more than one school, you'll notice that no two school cultures are identical. They may be similar but never identical. The culture within a school that operates in a high area of disadvantage may be markedly different to that of a leafy suburban school, but their end outcome may be similar – the very best outcomes.

What's the purpose of purpose?

Purpose acts as a vehicle to realise this same end outcome. A guiding force that serves and unites multiple individual purposes. Establishing a clear sense of purpose can:

- offer a clear rationale of why things are done in the way they are.
- offer a definition of what the school is 'about' and what 'the school stands for'.
- be a useful guiding force in times of challenge and when the going gets tough.
- be a useful guide to benchmark performance regularly.
- allow school teams to make difficult decisions by reviewing 'does this help us serve our purpose?'
- motivate staff to continue with the important work they do.

In their 2009 report 'School leadership and student outcomes: Identifying what works and why', Robinson, Hohepa and Lloyd synthesise the research between leadership and student outcomes. They identify eight dimensions of leadership practices and activities that lead to improved student outcomes, one of which is focused on establishing goals and expectations. Although the effect size was small, it was found to have an educationally significant impact on student outcomes. They describe establishing goals and expectations as 'setting, communicating and monitoring learning goals, standards and expectations'. Even more interestingly, they found some evidence that involvement of staff in the goal setting and reaching a 'consensus' around this was a key factor. In higher-achieving schools this was a result of leaders being focused on the 'goal' and making this a key priority and the staff aligning their practices to realise this goal.

The work from this synthesis emphasises the role that setting goals plays in raising student outcomes. Establishing a purpose is, in a sense, 'a goal'. For example, a school's purpose may be to 'enable pupils to be able to achieve their aspirations and flourish'. This is essentially the goal. But the word 'purpose' carries with it connotations of a more continual and sustained goal. In the context of education, it can also carry a moral imperative.

In 'Principled Curriculum Design' (2013) Dylan Wiliam zooms out and discusses the overarching purpose of education, outlining four broad categories:

1. Personal empowerment: to allow people 'to take greater control of their lives'.
2. Cultural transmission: to ensure people have cultural knowledge or 'the best that has been thought and known in the world' (Arnold & Wilson, 1969).
3. Preparation for citizenship: preparing people to make informed decisions in a democratic society.
4. Preparation for work: ensuring people achieve educationally and therefore prosper economically.

These categories provide useful direction in considering purpose in educational settings and the *why* of education.

So *why* else is it important to have a why? The importance of having a clear sense of purpose is supported by Dan Pink's work on motivation. In his book *Drive* (2009), Pink explores the role that purpose places in motivation. He refers to studies at MIT where a group of students were given a set of challenges (e.g. memorising digits and word puzzles) and were incentivised with varying degrees of reward. Essentially, if you did well, you got a larger cash prize. What did they find? If the task involved only mechanical skill, rewards were as expected. But when the task involved cognitive skill, the larger reward led to poorer performance. Pink was struck by this finding and, upon further research where the study was replicated by psychologists, sociologists and economists, concluded that when there's a complicated task at hand, we need more than just money to motivate. Pink asserts that there are three factors that lead to better performance: autonomy, mastery and purpose. More recently in 2017, Pink further embellishes the idea of purpose as purpose with a capital *P* and small *p* purpose. He defines small *p* purpose as personal and the small day-to-day acts and behaviours that make a difference. Contrastingly, purpose with a capital *P* is more large-scale and aspirational, e.g. achieving equity in education.

We have explored a few of the reasons why purpose is important in this chapter so far. Once an individual school's purpose has been defined, leaders can move their attention to *how* this is established and ultimately sustained (the arguably harder stuff!).

Case study: Communicating your purpose and what's required to fulfil it

Communicating purpose within any organisation is difficult to achieve with consistency and clarity. When embarking on new projects, policies or practices, leaders need to ensure that all staff know two things: *what* they are doing and *why* what they are doing matters. This information comes from having a clear strategy for communicating new initiatives, and a robust process of quality assurance that sits alongside it.

Communication is seen as the act of exchanging information with others through a variety of media. As a novice leader, I often relied on a communication medium that I was comfortable with presenting in front of staff or creating policy documentation. One of my biggest learning points, as I developed as a leader, was the importance of modelling. When launching a new way of producing curriculum maps with staff I led, I was anxious that departments were at different places with their understanding of this work. After following my preferred communication strategy of presenting to all staff, explaining why we were doing this work, and then producing a policy for creating these maps, I decided to engage in a process of modelling curriculum map creation. Rather than producing a single exemplar from one subject, working with subject experts allowed models to be created for each subject. This allowed for a more bespoke conversation around what I was asking staff to do.

Individual conversations with each department also led to a deeper understanding of why this work was so important. Communicating the purpose of the project was crucial for its success. Just as important was that this purpose was held centrally when the content of the curriculum maps were implemented in the classroom. For example, part of the purpose of this work was to have a greater focus on knowledge within the curriculum, and explicitly break down the knowledge that students need to know. This would need to be checked to ensure it was taking place, otherwise the purpose of the project had been missed. Therefore, quality assurance processes focused on whether the curriculum maps broke knowledge down into small enough chunks, and then whether knowledge was delivered in this way in the classroom. Where quality assurance identified that this was not taking place, swift action was delivered through live modelling as a supportive measure. It is crucial that staff understand that quality assurance is a supportive process, ensuring that what we all want done and why we want it to be done is clearly understood and consistently implemented. This demonstrates why quality assurance should be conducted by a subject expert. A robust programme of quality assurance has been a key feature of all successful plans that I have implemented. My experience has led me to some key questions I always consider when communicating the purpose of a project:

- Does the 'why' behind the 'what' they are doing make sense for every subject?
- Does 'what they are doing' look the same in every subject?
- How explicitly has the 'what' been modelled?

- How robustly has 'what' and 'why' been quality assured, both in planning and delivery?

Nimish Lad, trust-wide curriculum and research lead, former vice principal, @nlad84

Nimish Lad

Nimish's case study highlights the importance of communication, especially when communicating something as integral as purpose. Clarity of purpose can be the difference between people 'really getting it' and people 'superficially getting it'.

So what does a good one look like? In the first scenario (the best-case scenario), staff are clued up on the school's *why* and can readily articulate it. They can not only speak to the purpose but can also explain how what they do every day helps fulfil that purpose. They know their part in the wider 'machine' and understand both the macro and the micro (the big picture and the small details). In the second scenario (a less ideal situation), staff can 'parrot the purpose' but can't really explain it and don't understand how it relates to what they do day to day.

As discussed earlier, **being a part of the process of establishing and clarifying purpose can help teams to be more actively locked into the goal at hand. This is a delicate collaborative process and language is a key factor in essentially 'negotiating' this shared language.** At the heart of this process is conversation, which we will come to in chapter 4.

The English language is such that a single word can shift the tone and tenor of a message. Here we will explore language and how it enables us to connect our vision as leaders to a wider 'audience'.

Words matter

Language has brought people together since the beginning of time. From the cavemen who gathered around the fire and told each other stories, to the abbreviated acronyms we use to convey language over WhatsApp today. It's no surprise that language is critical when it comes to

A culture of purpose

A powerful idea but this does not negate the need for leaders to sometimes explicitly address the 'you' and how an individual's actions sit within the wider organisation. Context is king. If, for example, a teacher is reluctant to approach something in a way clearly defined by a school, a leader may have to be more explicit about the 'you' and how this impacts on consistency across the school or leads to a provision gap for pupils.

2

This may not be the intention but the connotation of language can alter perception and understanding.

3

A complete understatement of the dedication, emotional energy, physical energy, and commitment that goes into being a school leader.

establishing, communicating and repeatedly returning to a school's purpose.

In his book *Connect!*, Simon Lancaster, the prolific speechwriter, shares how we can create shared goals through simple language choices. He writes, 'one of the easiest ways for speechwriters to turn a "me" into a "we"[1] is by actively switching the pronoun from me to we… it's the difference between "you've all got to wear masks" and "we've all got to wear masks".… these connections can all help connect a "me" with a "we", connecting the personal with the collective, the specific with the universal.' Simple tweaks in the language we use can ensure that the goals we are setting and communicating are easily understood, shared endeavours.

This is only one example of how small tweaks to language can make a difference. There is, for example, a subtle but clear difference between communicating 'expectations' and 'non-negotiables'. When we communicate expectations, we're setting a clear parameter and raising aspirations. When we communicate non-negotiables, we unwittingly shut down conversations and diminish teachers' agency.[2] The impact of word choice isn't confined to generating 'buy-in' (for want of a better term). Having 'non-negotiables' can also implicitly encourage school leaders to fall foul of the sunk-cost fallacy, where people continue with a course of action due to the invested resources rather than it being the right call to make. This comes with the caveat that, in certain situations and contexts, non-negotiables may be required, but this example highlights why it's important for us to be intentional and considered in our language choices, particularly when communicating our 'why'.

What happens when purpose wanes?

The day-to-day running of a school is a tricky business. (Hats off to the school leaders reading this![3]) Earlier, I wrote about how purpose can be a guiding force and an 'anchor' in times of challenge. This is not an unusual occurrence in schools where the day-to-day operational running of schools can eclipse the 'core business' of school leaders. At times like this, purpose can wane.

Purpose, as articulated by a school, needs constant reinforcement to be successfully sustained. How do you go about achieving this? Referring to Bennett's 2017 report, we can find some useful guidance. Although specific to maintaining a strong culture of behaviour in schools, it offers excellent direction on how strong cultures in general are upheld and maintained.

One key recommendation offered for school leaders is designing social norms – behaviours that you would wish to see routinely throughout the school community. Social norms are a key part of our society and enable us to function and thrive as a collective. I argue that this idea holds value in our staff communities also. By setting 'social norms', aligned to our school's purposes, we are able to enact the purpose with our day-to-day behaviours. Over time, we inch closer towards fulfilling our purpose because the social norms that are instilled have become part and parcel of the daily life of the school. *'These routines should be communicated to, and practiced by, staff and students until they become automatic. This then frees up time, mental effort and energy towards more useful areas, such as study.'* So too can we design social norms for our professional communities that free up time and mental energy of educators to focus on the core business that is pupil achievement.

This, however, isn't enough to tackle a waning sense of purpose. The only way to truly attack this is by revisiting, repeatedly.[4]

Benett, 2017

4
Revisiting purpose needs to be followed by evaluating alignment to the shared purpose.

Case study: Michaela Community School

In October 2021, I visited the Michaela Community School in Wembley, known for its excellent academic outcomes despite the school's underprivileged demographic. I met with Katharine Birbalsingh, the headmistress of the school, to discuss how she sustains the strong school culture of high expectations and tradition. 'You have to keep reminding everyone' – Katharine spoke passionately about the importance of revisiting your purpose and the cultural/social norms of the school, not only until they were 'automatic' but beyond this.

| **A culture of purpose**

My experience of the school, having only visited for the day, made it clear that this repetitive revision of purpose and social norms was more than just lip service. The day-to-day routines were sharp. Not a minute was lost. Teachers and pupils could tell me about what the school culture was, what Michaela was about, and how things were done there. Unsurprisingly, everyone was on the same page.

What pleasantly surprised me, however, was the fact that this did not take away from the pupils' love for learning, socialising or enjoyment. It, if anything, strengthened it! Most importantly, the environment and pupils were regulated, allowing teachers to focus on the good stuff – the teaching and learning and giving their pupils the very best chance to succeed and flourish.

Pupils walked into the hall, reciting the poem If— by Rudyard Kipling. They did so proudly, with passion and a clear appreciation of the poetry. When I sat down to eat lunch with the pupils, the pupil at the head of the table served their peers (and me!), asking each, in turn, politely if they wanted water. This isn't an academic criterion, nor something that is tested in standardised examinations, but it is a human skill that will enable them to confidently dine with others – cultural transmission as Dylan Wiliam put it. There was purpose. It was tangible. And Ms Birbalsingh's role in maintaining this was clear.

I asked her how she ensures that the other senior leaders in her team were implementing the norms, enacting the school's vision and fulfilling its purpose. She said that she meets with her team *daily* to discuss the order of the day, to reinforce expectations and to check-in. It's easy to have aspirational and lofty vision in schools and an inspirational purpose, but making it happen is hard. This small ritual of morning SLT meetings shows how to keep the big picture purpose connected to the daily happenings within a school.

Replicating culture isn't the aim of this case study but what it does exemplify is how strong culture is sustained on the ground, in the most challenging of circumstances.

Summary

Having a clear and shared sense of purpose can unite school teams in the work they do day in, day out, providing staff at all levels with a sense of belonging to a shared endeavour. This sense of purpose can support in guiding the actions and decision-making in schools and can act as a guiding force for leaders when inevitably tough decisions need to be made.

Reflective questions for your school

1. As a school leader, have I explicitly shared the purpose of our work with my team?

2. How might I go about revisiting our shared sense of purpose?

3. How might I remind myself and others of our purpose during the day-to-day running of the school?

References

Arnold, M. and Wilson, J. D. (1969). *Culture and Anarchy.* Cambridge: Cambridge University Press.

Bennett, T. (2017). 'Creating a Culture: How school leaders can optimise behaviour'. Department for Education. Available at: bit.ly/2OV6bDy.

Lancaster, S. (2022). *Connect!: How to Inspire, Influence and Energise Anyone, Anywhere, Anytime.* London: Heligo Books.

Pink, D. H. (2009). *Drive: The Surprising Truth About What Motivates Us.* Edinburgh: Canongate Books.

Robinson, V. M. J., Hohepa, M. and Lloyd, C. (2009). School Leadership and Student Outcomes: Identifying What Works and Why Best Evidence Synthesis Iteration (BES). University of Auckland, Ministry of Education.

Wiliam, D. (2013). Principled Curriculum Design. London: SSAT.

| Chapter 3 | **A culture of trust** |

CHAPTERS

1	2	3	4	5	6	7	8
PAGE 15	PAGE 31	PAGE 45	PAGE 59	PAGE 69	PAGE 83	PAGE 95	PAGE 105

45

CHAPTER 3

A CULTURE OF TRUST

| **A culture of trust**

Trust can enhance the performance of a team.

Building and sustaining trust is not an easy business but one well worth investing in. Trust is an important mediator of collaboration, and it is only through authentic and whole-hearted collaboration that we can optimise the quality of education within our schools.

In chapter 1, the concept of psychological safety was explored. In chapter 2, that of purpose. Both are pre-requisites of strong school culture, but a golden thread that runs through all the conditions required for strong school culture is trust. In this chapter, the idea of trust and its important role in school leadership is further explored. Before doing so, I offer these important words from Simon Sinek (2020): 'Trust is built on telling people the truth, not telling people what they want to hear'.

The reason I chose these words to open the chapter is because, typically, as school leaders we fall foul of the misconception that trust is a by-product of 'being liked' and this becomes the core focus of our efforts. My craft experience as a senior leader, both working with and coaching other senior leaders, has taught me this – trust is crucial but if it's the kind of trust that is rooted in pleasing another, sometimes at the cost of candour and honesty, it's the wrong kind of trust.[1]

Let's begin with the definition of trust. There are, of course, different definitions. For this chapter, I will be referring to Solomon and Flores (2003): 'to trust is to take on the personal responsibility of making a commitment and choosing a course of action, and with it, one kind of relationship or another. Trust entails a lack of control, but it means entering a relationship in which control is no longer the issue. There is no need to broach the subject of trust with people or things that we can utterly control.'[2]

1
In chapter 7, we delve deeper into how trust is foundational to impactful feedback. In this chapter, we will go into more detail about why leaders need trust and how to cultivate it.

2
Essentially, trust requires a leap of faith. You must give it to get it, which as a leader can leave you feeling incredibly vulnerable. Vulnerability, contrary to popular belief, can strengthen relationships within teams.

What strikes me about this definition is that it included a recognition that trust occurs in equitable relationships where one individual does not have, or want, control of the other. For me, this definition is particularly pertinent when it comes to educational leadership and reinforces the work of Pink, Robinson and other colleagues who assert the importance of autonomy in leadership (both in the educational field and beyond).

Solomon and Flores (2003) highlight 'types' of trust and, quite logically, propose that 'blind trust' can be foolish and is problematic. Rather they suggest that trust is a mix of trust and distrust, or a sense that we're 'in this together' as a community. This does not mean school leaders should expect wholly trusting relationships with the staff they lead. It means they recognise that trust may be tentative, it may ebb and flow in the context of school life and in the face of adversity.

'Leadership trust is emotional and relational'

In Coe's (2022) research synthesis on school leadership, he refers to leadership trust as emotional and relational. A careful consideration of this can help shed light on what's necessary to develop what Solomon and Flores describe as authentic trust. Coe points to Tschannen-Moran and Hoy's (2000) definition of trust as 'the willingness to be vulnerable to another party based on the confidence that the latter party is benevolent, reliable, competent, honest and open'.

Coe goes on to explore trust through the lens of hierarchical dynamics within a school, referencing the work of Bryk et al (2010). He refers to downward trust (from principals to teachers) and upwards trust (from teachers to principals). Coe highlights the distinction made between these two types of trust, with downward trust 'depending more on a perception of competence and reliability' and upwards trust 'depending more on perceptions of integrity'. The evidence by Bryk et al (2010) shows that these measures predict future school improvement in student outcomes and are supportive mechanisms for improvement to take place.[3]

3
Coe states in the report that, all in all, the evidence base for educational leadership is not robust. It's important that when referencing this report, we remember that this is an evidence review of the existing research and the 'best bets' when it comes to educational leadership.

Take the hypothetical situation of a newly appointed deputy headteacher that is leading on curriculum in a school that requires drastic curriculum improvements. We can consider this scenario considering Bryk et al's work (2010). To mobilise the proposed curriculum changes they may be suggesting, the deputy headteacher must:

- establish a perception of competence and reliability with the headteacher.
- establish strong relationships with those they lead so that they are perceived to be operating with integrity.

This is no easy feat. It is complex and I don't claim to have the magic bullet for how this can be done. But an awareness of this can certainly guide the deputy's thinking, actions, and behaviour so that the curriculum work they are focused on has the maximum chance of success.

In this scenario, it is not merely a case of generating the two above criteria superficially and with a tick-list of 'to dos' rooted in being perceived as having integrity and competence. One cannot simply follow through on a few things and always appear 'smiley' to establish this trust. It is a case of consistent behaviours, rooted in these principles that, over time, lead to an understanding of this leader as a trustworthy and capable individual. This seems obvious but all too often, in multiple fields, leaders aim to 'manufacture' this kind of trust in a way that simply does not lend itself to the relational and emotional trust that Coe refers to. Another dimension of the definition of trust from Tschannen-Moran and Hoy (2000) is openness. Without a certain extent of transparency and openness, a relationship of trust simply cannot be negotiated. Simply put, you need to give it to get it. Therefore, trust is not only something which needs to be understood by school leaders but also enacted by school leaders. How does one go about achieving this in practice?

Yamina Bibi

Case study: Establishing trust

Being a new leader within any organisation comes with its challenges. Whenever I have taken on a new leadership role, whether it's been within my organisation or in a new organisation, I always feel anxious about how I will (re) establish myself as a leader so that I am able to build and maintain relationships based on trust, authenticity and credibility.

One of the ways I tried to limit the impact of this anxiety was by reading leadership books and blogs about how to build relational trust as a leader. I discovered Covey's *Speed of Trust* (2008) where he introduces the concept of the Four Cores of Credibility and explores how these help to increase relational trust in leaders. Integrity, intent, capabilities and results are key, Covey argues, in building trust within organisations. With this in mind, I thought carefully about how I could implement these. I started by getting to know colleagues by speaking to them about both work and non-work related topics during break time and lunch times and while passing them in the corridor. These 'micro moments' really helped to build a culture of care and, dare I say it, love amongst colleagues. By building relationships, I wanted colleagues to get to know me as well as me getting to know them. In doing so, it felt like an equal playing field in terms of honesty and vulnerability.

Another way in which I tried to implement Covey's Four Cores of Credibility was by sharing my vision, values and 'why' with the team regularly so that they always knew that any decisions made were driven by seeking success for students. By doing this, I hope that if I did decide that a colleague didn't align with these aspects, they would either understand why I chose this or challenge me.

I think a key part of building trust as a leader is about ensuring that others see our capabilities and trust our ability to be able to lead. Building domain specific knowledge can be key and Diana Osagie, an incredible leadership coach, taught me that even if we do not have the experience, we can gain theoretical knowledge by reading and reading some more. When I become senior leader in inclusion in a new school, I was incredibly worried because inclusion was not my expertise. So I read and attended lectures and courses and learned from the experts in my organisation and beyond. By focusing on developing my own capabilities and domain specific knowledge, I also found that I felt more confident. I would then share this knowledge to support colleagues through bulletins, briefings and CPD sessions. I also shared lessons and resources to share knowledge but also help reduce others' workload.

I found that colleagues appreciated the sharing of resources and trusted my knowledge as a result.

I did notice one consequence of my sharing. During a 360 evaluation I asked colleagues to do as part of a coaching course I was completing, colleagues were asked to rate on a scale of 100 whether I shared my areas of development and asked for help. The average for this was rated lower. I was initially shocked by this as I thought I did share my areas of development, but I realised that in my desire to prove myself and how 'good' I was at my job, I would not necessarily share my vulnerabilities. As a result of this, I began to share one or two of my areas of development in team meetings to help others share their vulnerabilities too and asked for help through delegation. I was careful about what I shared to build that trust as one of my coaches advised me that we don't need to always share everything with everyone.

At the end of the coaching course, colleagues were asked again whether I shared my areas of development and asked for help and this was rated higher. This is another way leaders can build trust by sharing some of their areas of development strategically so that colleagues know that you are also enhancing yourself in the same way you may be asking them to develop themselves.

All of this I found supported in building their trust in me as a leader but also of others too.

Trust is a tricky business

I've often found that large abstract concepts like trust are difficult to write about because in reducing their meaning into prose, you instantly reduce the complexity and subtlety of their very nature. We can conceptually attempt to define 'trust' but gaining and maintaining it is a very tricky business. Often, as school leaders, you must make tough decisions that may call into question people's trust of you. Those you lead may not have an awareness of all the contextual factors that led to a particular decision being made and there needs to be a recognition of this and an unrelenting drive to serve our purpose even when tough decisions do have to be made.

Viviane Robinson, professor at the University of Auckland, proposes that building relationships of trust is one of three key 'leadership capabilities' when solving the complex educational problem of school improvement. In her keynote paper, she explores these three capabilities in turn and refers to 'relational trust' and the interpersonal skills that school leaders employ and the findings related to these.

'Experienced school leaders know how to build relationships; what they find far more difficult is building and maintaining relationships of trust while addressing the difficult issues that are central to leading improvement.'

Robinson, 2017

Robinson references the work of Bryk and Schneider (2002) in the paper, who found that the daily interactions of leaders (their ability to demonstrate personal regard, interpersonal respect, competence, and personal integrity), impacted teachers' trust of those leaders. Robinson proposes that these elements be woven into research and development programmes to identify ways in which leaders can foster these. She suggests that a critical crossroad in maintain or breaking trust is presented when school leaders engage in performance-related conversations with those they lead. She highlights the conflict school leaders naturally experience between offering candid feedback and maintaining trust. This is a significant challenge when it comes to sustaining trust because conversations of this kind may not always be accepted as well-intentioned, thus compromising teacher's trust. In the next chapter, we explore how we can focus in on these types of conversations to ensure that they foster trust but also allow school leaders to chip away at the important business of school improvement.

Kate Stockings

Case study: How do you establish trust as a newly appointed leader?

Starting a new role as trust lead for geography in September meant that, for the third time in my career, I found myself with the exciting task of establishing trust with a new team. Having been at my previous school for four years and with a consistent geography teacher team for the duration, it had been a while since I had the opportunities (and challenges) that come with a 'fresh slate' – a new team of colleagues with which to build purposeful, authentic and effective relationships. In addition, this was my first move as an experienced leader where, having been a head of department for six years, I had experience of leadership and management to bring to the role (yet still with plenty more to learn, of course).

Before discussing and reflecting on establishing trust, it feels essential to share some context. After all, professional trust is so personal and contextual that to learn from each other we must be clear of the similarities and differences between our contexts. I think the following is essential background information before sharing my reflections:

- Firstly, I was starting in a new role as trust lead; the team of geographers had not worked with a trust lead before. This feels significant as it means that there was an absence of expectation based on how someone had previously done the role.

- Secondly, I had a 'profile' within the geography community thanks largely to Twitter but also from presenting CPD and writing published geography resources. I think this is important to acknowledge as many of the members of the geography teams knew something of my beliefs, approach and perspective with regards to geography education. This means that some may (or may not!) have already, to an extent, trusted me.

So, how did I seek to establish trust and what are my reflections? In a multi-school role where I don't spend every day with the geography teams, I knew that I needed to work carefully and thoughtfully to gain their trust as quickly as possible in order for us to collaborate effectively. If my work was going to be impactful, the geography team in each school needed to trust that I was working with the best intentions for both students and staff.

To achieve this, I had three initial ideas of how I would approach the first visit to each school and, feeling that they were working as I had hoped, these quickly became my three 'golden rules'. In the following paragraphs, I reflect on each rule and the impact that I believe it had.

I would meet everyone individually before observing them teach.

Although not ranked in significance, this rule might be the one that I felt had the biggest impact for establishing trust, and yet it is so simple. My rationale was clear: call it what you want, a drop-in, a learning walk or an observation is still another person passing some form of judgement (however low stakes) on your teaching. In a profession where issues of accountability and a lack of autonomy abound, I wanted to ensure that I was seen as more than just someone who dropped in on lessons, provided feedback and pointed out some future areas for improvement. I wanted to take my time to begin establishing the strong relationships that would ensure I am able to offer support, constructive feedback and professional challenge when and where needed, and all with integrity.

I was taken aback by how many of the staff were surprised by this approach. Whilst many teachers invited me straight into their classroom, a few asked me more nervously when I would be observing them. For anyone that asked or invited me into their classroom the answer was the same: I wouldn't be observing or dropping in on anyone before I had spoken to them and introduced myself properly first. Whilst this did mean that the start of the role felt a little slower in pace than might have otherwise been achieved (it took until the end of half term 1 to undertake observations in each of the schools), I think the benefits far outweigh any negatives.

Certainly, this is a simple rule that I will carry forward with me into all future leadership roles. I would argue that this approach to those initial meetings and observations enabled me to cultivate trust that has led to subsequent observation feedback being far more impactful as a result.

I would meet individually with each teacher to find out more about their professional identity, motivations and aspirations.

The importance of doing this to build professional trust is something that I learned the hard way. When I first took over as head of department, I naively assumed that everyone in the team was like me: a geographer who adored their subject and whose motivation for teaching is largely grounded in a love of geography. My assumption was that everyone identified professionally as a geographer, was motivated to engage with geography education more broadly, and aspired to becoming a head of geography themselves. I can now recognise that this was ridiculous on my part; something I realised through setting aside the time to purposefully speak to each teacher and unpack their professional identity. I now know how different teacher identities can be.

Some colleagues will have other roles in the school and, therefore, see geography as the means through which to deliver the classroom teaching element of their role. Some colleagues will see geography as the lens through which they teach students but they identify as teachers of children before they are teachers of geography. To put it simply, not everyone will think about education and their role the same way that you do.

CHAPTERS

1	2	**3**	4	5	6	7	8	**55**
PAGE 15	PAGE 31	**PAGE 45**	PAGE 59	PAGE 69	PAGE 83	PAGE 95	PAGE 105	

How does this relate to trust? I would argue that once you have given someone the time to share their professional identity, motivations and aspirations, it is much easier for them to trust that you are working with them to achieve your common goal of improving education. You might both have different ambitions and motivations but you're working towards that same goal.

I would explain why I had taken the role and what I was hoping to achieve in the medium term.

This is perhaps of particular importance for a multi-school role where there is a risk that you could appear as be 'doing things to' staff rather than 'doing things with' them. So, I made sure that I explained a little bit about myself to everyone in each school's geography team. I explained that having been head of department for six years, I now wanted the opportunity to engage with my subject on a broader scale, working across a number of schools to improve the provision of geography for as many students as possible. I explained that I adore teaching my subject and wanted to have the headspace away from all of the other elements of full-time school life to think critically about geography curriculum, pedagogy and assessment. In other words, I explained that the reason I was in the role was to help us all aim for the very best geography teaching possible.

Through giving this broader context, I think that colleagues were able to trust my aims and intentions more quickly. They trusted (hopefully) that I was undertaking the role with the best intentions and that I was working to the same goal as them: the best geography education possible. Again, this is not a complex approach to building trust but I wonder how often you've had a middle or senior leader explain their motivation to you. Whilst many headteachers introduce themselves in this way when first arriving at a school, it is (in my experience) far rarer from people in other senior or middle leader roles.

| Chapter 3 | # A culture of trust |

Summary

Trust takes time to establish but is important in developing the relational foundations from which strong and sustainable school improvement flourishes. To develop trust, we often need to offer a level of trust and 'vulnerability'. Ongoing dialogue and conversation are at the heart of these exchanges.

Reflective questions for your school

1. Is there a culture of trust within my school? How might I accurately gauge this?

2. What can I do to promote a culture of trust within the school?

3. How might I navigate a situation where trust has been lost? How can conversation play a role in this?

References

Bryk, A. S., Sebring, P. A., Allensworth, E. and Luppescu, S. (2010). Organizing Schools for Improvement: Lessons from Chicago. Chicago: University of Chicago Press.

Bryk, A. S. and Schneider, B. (2002). Trust in Schools: A Core Resource for Improvement. New York: Russell Sage Foundation.

Coe, R. (2022). 'School Environment and Leadership: Evidence Review' Evidence Based Education

Covey, S. (2008). The Speed of Trust. New York: Free Press.

Robinson, V. (2017). Capabilities required for leading improvement: Challenges for researchers and developers. University of Auckland, Research Conference 2017.

Robinson, V., Hohepa, M. and Lloyd, C. (2009). School Leadership and Student Outcomes: Identifying What Works and Why Best Evidence Synthesis Iteration (BES).

Sinek, S. [@simonsinek] (2020). Trust is built on telling the truth, not telling people what they want to hear. [Tweet]. Twitter. bit.ly/3G16hat.

Solomon, R. C. and Flores, F. (2003). Building Trust: In Business, Politics, Relationships, and Life. Oxford: Oxford University Press.

Tschannen-Moran, M. and Hoy, W. K. (2000). 'A Multidisciplinary Analysis of the Nature, Meaning, and Measurement of Trust', Review of Educational Research, 70(4).

CHAPTERS

1	2	3	4	5	6	7	8
PAGE 15	PAGE 31	PAGE 45	PAGE 59	PAGE 69	PAGE 83	PAGE 95	PAGE 105

57

| Chapter 4 | **A culture of conversation** |

CHAPTERS

| 1 | 2 | 3 | 4 | 5 | 6 | 7 | 8 | **59** |
| PAGE 15 | PAGE 31 | PAGE 45 | **PAGE 59** | PAGE 69 | PAGE 83 | PAGE 95 | PAGE 105 | |

CHAPTER 4

A CULTURE OF CONVERSATION

Conversations can be a strong mediator of school improvement.

In a fascinating research paper exploring belief validity testing in conversations between educational leaders and staff, Sinnema et al (2021) analysed 43 conversations to investigate educational leaders' problem-solving attempts and what influences these attempts. They concluded that these attempts were influenced by 1) beliefs about the nature of the problem 2) what causes it and 3) how to solve it. They also found that 'leaders tended to avoid discussion of problem causes, advocate more than inquire, bypass disagreements, and rarely explore logic between solutions and problem causes.' They concluded that patterns uncovered in their research are likely to impact whether problems – micro or macro – are ultimately solved. They suggest a nested model of educational problem solving, as seen in figure 1 (rooted in the work of Bronfenbrenner's ecological systems theory), that illustrates the different levels of system problems from micro to chrono.

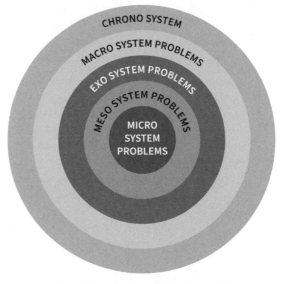

Figure 1: Nested model of educational problem solving

They assert that leaders' effectiveness in discussion about micro problems considerably impacts the success of larger exo system problems and, in turn, the macrosystem. Essentially, the little things count. This demonstrates the important role conversation and problem-solving plays in our wider education system.

This study highlights why conversations are crucial and how tricky it is to get conversations right as an educational leader. However, it also highlights the 'sticking points' that may present difficulties within these conversations that can act as a useful reference point for leaders. An awareness of these sticking points alone may allow leaders to take a considered approach to their conversations and aim to mitigate against these.

The work of Viviane Robinson, where she empirically examines the impact of leadership on student outcomes, identified five dimensions of student-centred leadership which have the most impact on student outcomes. These are:

1. Establishing goals and expectations
2. Resourcing strategically
3. Ensuring quality teaching
4. Leading teacher learning and development
5. Ensuring an orderly and safe environment

High-quality, intentional conversations are key

Each of these five strands has something in common: the need for high-quality, intentional conversations. Yet, as we explored in the previous chapter, conversations – particularly those related to performance or feedback – can be significantly challenging for school leaders. The reality remains that these conversations are necessary for school improvement and, therefore, the art of the conversation becomes integral to school improvement. How do we address this when developing school leaders at all levels? How can school leaders have successful conversations that allow for a focus on improved outcomes for pupils, whilst still maintaining strong interpersonal relationships within their teams?

I propose that 'conversations for possibilities' can be a useful tool in every leader (and teachers') toolkit, when engaging in dialogue of any kind. Here we will explore the different types of conversations and how they can be utilised to meet goals within our schools. 'Conversations for possibilities' are described as conversations where possibilities are declared and that go on to be fulfilled inside of a 'conversation for action'. These conversations, therefore, answer the question, 'how might we reach our collective goal?' and encourages collaboration of the truest kind (Flores, 2013).

Fernando Flores and his colleague Terry Winograd (1988) suggest four categories of conversation during their work in the 1980s, which offer a useful framework from which to explore types of conversations:

1. Conversations for action (a request that may then be committed to or disregarded).
2. Conversations for clarification (clarifying something already declared).
3. Conversation for possibilities (exploring possibilities).
4. Conversation for orientation (exchanging information).

Although there seems a logical order by which a leader would generally have these conversations (orientation first, then possibilities, action, and clarification), this may not be the most useful way to consider these conversation types. For example, there may be occasions where leaders must have conversations for action due to time constraints and contextual factors.

Rather we can consider these types of conversations in terms of when they may be appropriate, the kind of language that may be used to support these conversations, and the implications of these on school culture and ultimately school improvement. The table that follows summarises this.

Type of conversation	School topic of conversation suited to type of conversation	Language you may wish to use	Reflective questions to consider before engaging in conversation
All school-based conversations must start and end with 'how does this impact pupil outcomes?' A useful question to pose at the end of every conversation is 'so what..?' What now? What next? How does this impact pupil outcomes?			
Conversation for action	• Implementation of any kind e.g., behaviour interventions, curriculum model, assessment model. • Revisiting intention and vision (to strongly associate to day-to-day action on the ground).	• Our collective goal is… • The expectation will be that… • The purpose of this is… • We will review the impact/success of this and review at this time… • This is something we need to go 'all in on'.	• Is this the right time of the day/term/year to be having this conversation? • What has been the rate of change at this school recently? Might that impact the conversation? • What has been the success rate of previous conversations I've had about X, Y and Z? How might I change my tack? • What would be the least ideal/most ideal outcome from this conversation for both parties? • How can I accurately gauge whether information has been clearly communicated after the conversation?
Conversation for clarification	• Overall roles and responsibilities: who does what and how. • Clarifying expectations. • Lesson learned from implementation and clarifying future actions based on this.	• We are collectively trying to achieve X and need to keep this in mind… • A lesson learned from the past term is ____. Going forward we can ____ to address this. • Just as a helpful reminder, X is leading on ____, Y is leading on ____ and this is who you need to go to if you're unsure.	

| **A culture of conversation**

Type of conversation	School topic of conversation suited to type of conversation	Language you may wish to use	Reflective questions to consider before engaging in conversation
All school-based conversations must start and end with 'how does this impact pupil outcomes' – a useful question to pose at the end of every conversation is 'so what..?' What now? What next? How does this impact pupil outcomes?			
Conversation for possibilities	• Curriculum/ assessment model review. • Exploring ways of working during implementation of any kind. • Proposing ideas ('managing' upwards for teachers) or course-correcting (when adjusting implementation).	• I wonder if we could… • What would happen if… • Let's play devil's advocate… what could go wrong here? • How could we/ might we…? • What might be the unintended outcomes of this?	• What might I do to confirm what's been agreed as an aide-mémoire for both parties after the conversation? • Time of day/time of term/time of year. • How can I make this feel less *judgemental* and more *developmental*?
Conversation for orientation	• Action planning. • Curriculum audit. • Subject leader accountability: what has been done, when and why, and its impact/ next steps. • Prioritising foci for term/year.	• What are the key headlines? • What's the top three things I need to know about this? • What's the top three takeaways I want the other party to leave with after this conversation?	

Now, in reality, it's very difficult to group conversations into neatly wrapped boxes which come with guidance manuals to support leaders, or indeed teachers, in having these conversations. The table, however, can offer a very broad and general mental model to allow colleagues to consider more deeply the conversations they are having, why they are having them, and how these directly impact student outcomes. I will offer two examples of how this table could be used to support school-based conversations:

CHAPTERS

1	2	3	**4**	5	6	7	8	**65**
PAGE 15	PAGE 31	PAGE 45	**PAGE 59**	PAGE 69	PAGE 83	PAGE 95	PAGE 105	

one in which a curriculum leader is exploring the school's assessment model and has a conversation with the headteacher, and one where a headteacher is meeting with a head of science to discuss their end of year outcomes. Of course, these conversations don't capture the level of detail or nuance in terms of reaction and emotion that a 'real' conversation would, but they hopefully offer a bit of context around how a conversation for possibility might unfold and the impact using these language scaffolds may have on the tone of these meetings.

Example 1: Conversation for possibility with the headteacher

I am an assessment lead who is looking to move towards a renewed assessment model at my school (a secondary school) for the next academic year. I felt like what was currently in place wasn't really working and we needed to move to a model that focused on assessment that truly informs the curriculum and how it's enacted. We had just finished a round of assessments and teachers had spent considerable time analysing the data. Through my conversations with teachers and subject leaders, it was clear that this process was an onerous one and that teachers were finding it challenging to use the data in a meaningful way, due to several reasons. Acting as a key bit of evidence to justify a potential move to a new assessment model within the school, I went to go speak to the headteacher about this. We had already met prior to this meeting about the data headlines from the assessments. During this meeting, we had discussed the concerns around assessment and I explained that I would be bringing a proposed assessment model to our next meeting to go through. I began by laying out the challenges associated with the current model and then moving into a proposed model. The following summarises the kind of language I used in the conversation to explore the possibilities.

'As we discussed in the last meeting, I think perhaps we need to look into moving to an assessment model that tackles the issue of workload and is more meaningful for teachers. I looked at different models used across the trust to draw on best practice and I wonder if we could explore X model from X school… If we were to adopt this model, we might wish to consider… Playing devil's advocate, the issue we might come across in our context is… To get around this we could either a) adapt the model by… b) adopt a similar model that takes this into account.'

Example 2: Headteacher meeting with head of science to discuss end of year outcomes

'First of all, let's take the time to celebrate the wins from this year, what would you say you're most proud of? These are great achievements and it's important to recognise these and understand that, in the context we've been operating in, these are crucial wins. Let's explore the headline data….'

'I wonder if … has been a factor in terms of the outcomes for this particular group. What do you think?'

'How might we adapt this going forward? Playing devil's advocate, this is likely to be a challenge for us next year too because …, so it's an important one to consider.'

'I really like this suggestion because it tackles… How might we ensure this has a direct impact on student outcomes?'

'What might be the unintended outcome of moving in this direction in the science department? Is there anything we could do to mitigate against it?'

Summary

Conversations and dialogue are the basis for all types of school improvement. Through conversation, we're able to establish trust, share school improvement priorities and navigate the complexities involved in responding to these priorities. The quality of these conversations can impact the quality of implementation and, therefore, it's important for school leaders to consider how these conversations are being conducted, the language they use and how aligned actions are to these conversations.

Reflective questions for your school

1. How often do conversations take place in my school? What kinds of conversations are taking place?

2. How are important conversations about the core business of teaching and learning structured? How do these conversations translate into action?

3. What could I do as a school leader to support high-quality, rich dialogue about teaching and learning?

References

Flores, F. (2013). *Conversations for Action and Collected Essays.* CreateSpace Independent Publishing Platform.

Robinson, V. (2011). Student-centered leadership (Vol. 15). San Francisco: Jossey-Bass.

Sinnema, C., Meyer, F., Le Fevre, D. (2021). 'Educational leaders' problem-solving for educational improvement: Belief validity testing in conversations', *Journal of Educational Change*, doi. org/10.1007/s10833-021-09437-z.

Winograd, T. (1988). 'A Language/Action Perspective on the Design of Cooperative Work', *Computer-Supported Cooperative Work: A Book of Readings*, 623-653.

| Chapter 5 | **A culture of rethinking** |

CHAPTER 5

A CULTURE OF RETHINKING

Rethinking can support teams to respond and innovate in the face of challenge.

Grant, 2021

'Most of us take pride in our knowledge and expertise, and in staying true to our beliefs and opinions. That makes sense in a stable world, where we get rewarded for having conviction in our ideas. The problem is that we live in a rapidly changing world, where we need to spend as much time rethinking as we do thinking.'

Rethinking allows us to learn from implementation, refine our approaches and change course when necessary. It safeguards us of falling foul to the sunk-cost fallacy and enables us as leaders to model continuous professional learning.

The conditions and tools shared thus far that can impact school improvement remain inconsequential without the domain-specific focus on high-quality teaching and learning. Viviane Robinson emphasises the importance of a focus on the 'core business of teaching and learning' so that leaders can maximise their positive influence on student outcomes. And so, the focus in this chapter will be on the power of rethinking and how it can be tied into curriculum implementation.

In his book *Think Again: The Power of Knowing What You Don't Know*, organisational psychologist Adam Grant offers a comprehensive view of why rethinking is so integral to success in organisations: 'Most of us take pride in our knowledge and expertise, and in staying true to our beliefs and opinions. That makes sense in a stable world, where we get rewarded for having conviction in our ideas. The problem is that we live in a rapidly changing world, where we need to spend as much time rethinking as we do thinking.' As a leader at any level, this idea will perhaps resonate with you.

Multiple factors influence what happens within a school. Some factors are less within educators' control, such as national reform, and others are more localised within individual schools. Amidst these constantly shifting sands, leaders have the difficult task of maintaining a consistent 'drumbeat' through both the declarative of their vision and the enacting of this vision day to day. This is the very nature of what makes decision-making in schools so complex and why rethinking can be such a helpful tool.

Mary Myatt (2022), a leading authority on curriculum in the UK, often talks about how 'it's never a blame game' when it comes to school improvement. I would argue that this is a crucial prerequisite of the concept of rethinking in our schools.

Rethinking in schools is a process

Often when an idea, initiative or intervention goes awry, more energy is lost through various parties fretting about harsh accountability measures, professional rollockings, and a sense of embarrassment or shame. Rather, this time could be spent rethinking. This might involve:

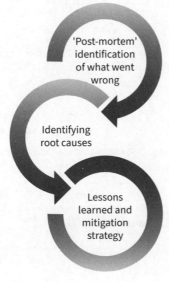

Figure 1: Rethinking in schools

'Post-mortem' analysis may seem quite morbid, but the construct is an exceptionally useful way of rethinking a situation. The idea is that if a decision is made, and an intervention is implemented and it goes horribly wrong, then leaders spend time with their teams, exploring where and how it went wrong to a) decide on the best course of action going forward and b) prevent it from happening again.

The idea isn't revolutionary but often not enough time is dedicated to this process in schools. The realities and pace of school life mean that before we've had a chance to catch our breath and engage in the reflective process of rethinking, we're already considering our next implementation project. This can be problematic and lead to an endless cycle of wasted resource, futile implementation, and frustrated staff.

I asked Karren Knowlton, an organisational psychologist, about 'rethinking' in the context of education.

Karren Knowlton

Q&A with Karren Knowlton

1. In education, the moral imperative and desire to achieve the best for our pupils quickly can sometimes mean that leaders might avoid rethinking. What are the key reasons you would provide in terms of the benefits of rethinking?

   Rethinking allows us to unlearn false beliefs and develop ever more accurate views of the world – the key benefits are a more accurate understanding of everything around us, which also means we can adapt more easily as the world changes, help others to do the same, and ultimately build cultures that are more flexible and resilient.

2. How can educational leaders avoid the many biases that can reduce the accuracy and thus impact of our decision-making?

   The biggest first step is learning what those biases are and how they operate. They're all different and there's no silver bullet for continual education, which is what rethinking is all about. *Thinking, Fast and Slow* by

Kahneman is a great primer. You might also check out *Decisive* by the Heath brothers.

3. How can educational leaders reconcile the need to appear confident and offer clarity to those they lead and the need to rethink to ensure robust decision making?

   They can role model confident humility, as Adam Grant discusses in *Think Again* – being confident in your tools and your ability to find answers and paths forward, even if that means questioning your current approach.

4. What would you say are the top three things that could benefit educational leaders from the world of organisational psychology?

   The Culture Code by Dan Coyle and *The Fearless Organization* by Amy Edmonson can help speak to this.

There are visible by-products and root causes

The Education Endowment Foundation's implementation guidance offers a valuable resource to support implementation efforts in schools and acts as useful guidance in supporting leaders with their thinking and decision-making. The report explores the process of implementation and offers a model where implementation can broadly be split into four parts:

Figure 2: EEF Implementation Guidance

Here, I will focus on the exploration phase. Mostly because my lived experience as a senior leader has taught me this exploration phase is far from simple and, if we don't get it right (which happens!), it has implications for the rest of the implementation phases, inevitably leading to de-implementation down the line, which further depletes hard-won time and energy. We also need to lay the cards on the table and accept that although this isn't ideal, it is a reality and when this situation occurs, as with all errors, the best we can do is approach a 'lessons learned' stance to refine our professional toolkit for future implementation.

Ideally, we would want to get this exploration phase as right as possible so that we can identify a well-informed 'best bet' and pour resource into the right place, maximising our chances of having meaningful impact on pupils in classrooms. Let's start by thinking about the *purpose* of the explore phase. Inspired by the Frayer Model, let us begin by looking at what the purpose *is not*. It is not to:

- place blame or poke holes in practice.
- solely pick out problems.
- inform a well-written document that will be sent to various stakeholders to affirm confidence in the leader's perceived expertise.
- be seen to be 'exploring' the state of play for a decision already made by senior leaders.

The purpose of the explore phase is to engage in a school-wide, collaborative consideration of an element of practice, with the shared goal of developing an accurate picture of where practice currently sits and what can be done to support improvement in this area, both at a surface level (addressing the visible by-products) and the root causes (the systems, structures, and underlying approaches).

I place emphasis on this distinction between the by-products and root causes because, quite often, the former overpowers the latter. For example, if reading progress isn't where it needs to be (the visible by-product), there are multiple potential root causes. The explore phase allows us to gather evidence of what the root cause is most likely to be so that we can choose a course of action that will address the issue at hand.

A word of warning here…

Hierarchical 'I'm big, you're small' Trunchbull-style assessments of 'what is good' and 'what is bad' in this explore phase will likely further compound the situation. If collective improvement is to be seen, collective understanding needs to be developed. I'm not contesting that subject specialists or senior leaders should not lead this body of work, but I am very aware that often this explore phase can become a 'mini Ofsted-style assessment' of practice, which damages the foundations of school improvement – a continuous culture of improvement. Damaging this is not the way to go. Engaging in conversation with teachers and support staff on the ground, collating and corroborating perspectives, evidence and sources of information is the best way to build an *accurate* view of both the priority that needs to be addressed and what is leading to the challenges in this area in the first place.

One without the other is inconsequential. Knowing you have a problem without understanding the root cause isn't going to resolve the problem, and understanding the root cause without knowing what it leads to renders us unable to measure whether our theory of change is having tangible impact when addressed.

Stories are central to thinking and rethinking

In *The Perils of Perception* by Bobby Duffy (2019), a key recommendation put forth for managing our misconceptions is that we need to tell the story: 'Although facts are important, they are not sufficient given how our brains work. We need to be aware of how people hear and use these, turning them into stories that might not always lead to the right conclusions. There is no contradiction between facts and stories; you don't need to choose one to make your point. The power of stories over us means we need to engage people with both.'

This quote highlights the co-existence of both qualitative and quantitative information in crafting an accurate picture of the state of play of something in question.

One last thing that I feel is crucial to consider when exploring is a recognition that no matter who we are and what level of 'expertise' we hold, you don't know what you don't know (she says, sheepishly, writing this book). Adam Grant writes about this extensively in *Think Again*. The visual in figure 3, adapted from his book, summarises it nicely. We mitigate against this one in the same way we mitigate against damaging culture within schools – collaboration over competition, development over judgement and an unrelenting sense of purpose to the pupils we serve.

WHAT I KNOW

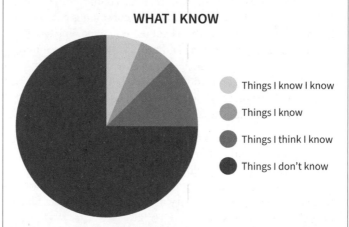

Things I know I know

Things I know

Things I think I know

Things I don't know

Figure 3: Adapted from *Think Again*, Adam Grant (2021)

Alison Peacock

Case study: Rethinking curriculum

A curriculum for learning without limits

As a school leader I was engaged in research with the University of Cambridge that built upon my participation in a groundbreaking study about the limitations of differentiation, *Learning without Limits* (2004). I accepted the post of headteacher in a primary school with nursery where the curriculum on offer was moribund. Teachers felt paralysed by an Ofsted judgement of special measures; attainment was at rock bottom and all aspects of the school were subject to extreme regular scrutiny. I had no choice other than to embrace curriculum renewal as part of the route towards school improvement, instinctively I knew that the way to raise attainment in core subjects would be to value, nurture and celebrate learning across all curriculum domains.

Over time, the school achieved many accolades. The first of these was that, after moving off special measures within a year, we were also recognised in the top 100 of schools that had most improved in school test performance. The Reggio Emilia approach to early years settings values the environment as 'the third teacher'. Influenced by this, I worked with local artists, art students, and the children and teachers to create wonderful pieces of art to 'lift' the feeling of the school. This impacted the overall impression of the school as a centre of learning with the highest ambition where intellectual achievement was noted and celebrated, and where anything might be possible.

Leadership of a full diverse and dynamic curriculum is complex. In a one-form entry school there simply are not enough bodies to individually lead curriculum areas. As the school developed, we approached everything through a lens of 'collective endeavour', thereby amplifying our capacity. It was with this in mind that we decided to divide the full curriculum offer into three faculty teams. Each faculty included teachers, student teachers, teaching assistants, governors and wider team members and parents who had a particular interest or specialism to contribute. The teams were:

Humanities: history, geography, global education and sustainability, languages, design and technology, maths.

Creative: play, music, dance, drama, English, computing, art.

Health and wellbeing: forest school, extended school, lunchtime play, religious education, RSHE, science, physical education and games.

A culture of rethinking

At twilight faculty team meetings, we set about telling the story of each subject area from nursery through to year 6. We gathered evidence and built A2 portfolios of curriculum plans and the ways they were enacted. This celebratory process helped all colleagues to recognise connections and see where gaps needed to be filled. We also included the children as we sought to evaluate what our school offered. Through initiatives such as whole school circle groups, we collated feedback about favourite books, mathematical thinking, visits, philosophical debate and much more. Children contributed to whole school films that illustrated our approach to curricular provision in specific subjects such as history or mathematics. This was an ongoing lively collaborative process that meant colleagues felt empowered to talk about development of subjects across ages and throughout classes with constant access to ongoing evaluative material that illustrated impact.

One of the core ways that current inspection teams evaluate the impact of the curriculum is by talking with children about what they can recall of their learning. In a school where building metacognitive strength is at the heart, such conversations are richly enjoyed by the children. Instead of worrying about what the adult means by their questioning, the child is much more likely to enthusiastically share their learning because they are constantly involved in evaluating their own progress over time. During one of our most recent inspections, a lead inspector commented that he could hardly walk through the playground without children bombarding him with their experiences of how they embraced learning challenges.

The core pillars of a teacher's role encompass curriculum, pedagogy and assessment. If the teacher provides a classroom environment where there is a constant focus on not only *what* the children are learning but *how* this is taking place, with emphasis on children illustrating progress and reflecting on this over time, then we have classrooms where every child is both learning and assessing constantly. Consolidating the child's skills to self-assess and to draw connections between past and current study is optimised when the school engages children in review events such as parent consultations and report writing. This formalises the assessment process and encourages the school community to see progress as a continuum rather than a fixed attainment point.

As a headteacher, I joined learning review meetings twice a year with all year 5 and year 6 children, their teachers and parents. These meetings were an opportunity for children to review their most recent learning and to illustrate this through a PowerPoint presentation of challenges and successes. Additionally, we would look through the children's books as they talked about what was going well and where they needed extra help. Each appointment was held in my office with the child seated at my desk leading the meeting. I took notes of each meeting and these built over the two year monitoring period. This ensured that we had a record of learning challenges and successes and that, between meetings, we acted on areas where the child particularly requested extra support or opportunities.

Additionally, children throughout the school typed their learning successes and challenges across the full curriculum into an end of report document. Photographs were added from the class blog and teachers responded with their qualitative assessment of progress achieved. As headteacher, I added a final comment alongside parental feedback at the end of the report. Very young children conferenced with older peers so that their comments could be typed in. These reports not only formed an important record of learning but also reinforced for every child the importance of being able to carefully reflect on progress that was taking place. Children enjoyed looking back through all their written work across the year in preparation for summative comments.

'Learning without limits' as a philosophy is about ensuring that 'a way through' is found for every individual and that children always have the opportunity to surprise themselves and others with their achievements. Offering the broadest possible curriculum and ensuring that successes are noted in all areas ensures that the school is able to provide an irresistible offer for all.

Summary

Rethinking is central to 'getting it right', something that as school leaders we're all keen to do. In complex school environments where multiple factors impact quality of education, it's crucial that as leaders we have the humility and the insight to be able to readily rethink so that we don't get caught in a sunk-cost fallacy, where we 'stick to our guns' even if we know an avenue of decision-making isn't quite having the impact that we thought it would.

Reflective questions for your school

1. What mechanisms are in place in my school for teachers and colleagues to rethink?

2. How do I work with my senior leader team in a way that enables regular rethinking?

3. What are the costs of rethinking and how might I manage this should I need to change the course of action over time?

References

Duffy, B. (2019). *The Perils of Perception: Why We're Wrong About Nearly Everything*. London: Atlantic Books.

Education Endowment Foundation. (2019). Putting Evidence to Work: A school's guide to implementation, [Report], bit.ly/3ttej4w.

Grant, A. (2021). *Think Again: The Power of Knowing What You Don't Know*. New York: Viking.

Hart, S., Drummond, M. J., Dixon, A. and McIntyre, D. (2004). *Learning without Limits*. Maidenhead: Open University Press.

Myatt, M. [@MaryMyatt] (2022). 'If schools have identified that some pupils are not being read to at home (this is never a blame game) they might want to consider the impact of the 'Just Reading' research /3', [Tweet], bit.ly/3TB56ld.

CHAPTERS

1	2	3	4	5	6	7	8
PAGE 15	PAGE 31	PAGE 45	PAGE 59	PAGE 69	PAGE 83	PAGE 95	PAGE 105

81

| Chapter 6 | **A culture of flex** |

CHAPTER 6

A CULTURE OF FLEX

Chapter 6	A culture of flex

Flexing is essential for us to be context-considerate.

A 'tight but loose' culture of flex aligns perfectly with the idea of evidence-informed practice. It recognises clear parameters or 'best bets' but allows for context-dependent manoeuvre sthat empowers teachers to lean into their craft expertise too.

Schools cannot function without adequate and robust systems and processes. When clearly set out, these systems allow leaders and teachers to focus on the important work of school improvement, rather than being caught up in operational chaos.[1] Above these necessary systems and processes is a layer of intentional choices made around teaching, learning, assessment, and curriculum aimed at more directly improving pupil outcomes.

The implementation of these curriculum models can be approached in various ways and are influenced by several factors unique to each individual school. A consideration that leaders may wish to make when focusing their attention on implementation is the concept of 'tight but loose', first brought to the educational context by Dylan Wiliam. In this chapter, we will explore this concept and how it may support leaders in cultivating a culture of flex, where teachers are autonomous professionals but whole teams can still 'row together' to achieve collective goals.

In my conversations with newly emerging and trust-wide leaders, achieving this balance between autonomy and uniformity consistently arises as a persistent challenge. This is true particularly in the context of curriculum – the substance of what goes on in schools day to day. Teaching is, by its very nature, a creative profession and no teacher enters the profession with the hope of being provided a dense textbook on their subject and being asked to deliver it verbatim. At the same time, we cannot expect pupils to flourish with patchy and inconsistent curricular quality year

1
Much like the cognitive load we refer to in pupils' learning.

on year and varying expectations around what knowledge 'should' be delivered.

The acceleration of educational research and evidence-informed practices in the last decade has prompted an increasingly considered approach to pedagogy. This means teachers are working harder than ever around *how* they are delivering content to maximise the chances of learning – 'a change in pupil's long-term memory'. I would argue that the cognitive load associated with both this and the *what* of the curriculum (what is being taught) is far too much in terms of workload for teachers. If teachers are expected to have a sharp focus on both, we risk the quality of teaching and learning being significantly diminished.

I would argue that a culture of flex is a considered solution to this complex problem. With clear parameters around what needs to be taught and an offer of high-quality curricular resources to support the delivery of this, teachers are empowered with the mental capacity to navigate the complexities of the exposition. This is a fine balance and one that needs to be negotiated carefully.

The concept of 'tight but loose' has been studied extensively by organisational psychologist Michele Gelfand at Stanford University over the past couple of decades, specifically to uncover the role that rules, culture, and norms play in our lives. Her work highlights why some cultures are 'tight', indicating stronger norms, and some are 'loose' with weaker norms. Interestingly, she found that countries that experienced considerably more threat (in the form of natural disasters, famine, etc) were tighter. Essentially, countries that faced more threat felt the need for more order and for rules. But like most decisions, tight cultures and loose cultures are subject to opportunity-cost.

In tight cultures, although there is more order and organisation, there is less openness and less creativity. In loose cultures there is more freedom and scope for new ideas, but this comes at a cost: disorganisation and frustration often accompany it.

In the paper 'Tight but Loose: A Conceptual Framework for Scaling Up School Reforms' by Marnie Thompson and

Dylan Wiliam (2008), they apply the concept of tight but loose to school reforms, specifically in terms of scaling up a classroom-based intervention. They aptly point out that 'no one else can do teachers' teaching for them, just as no one else can do students' learning for them. No matter how good an intervention's theory of change or how well designed its components, the design and implementation effort will be wasted if the intervention does not actually improve teachers' practices—in all the diverse contexts in which they work. This is the challenge of scaling up.'

This brings to the fore some important considerations. The idea that no one can do teachers' teaching for them is of particular interest and highlights a very real challenge around providing high-quality professional learning for teachers. Practioners who provide professional learning for teachers simply cannot 'do' teaching for teachers. The best they can do is equip teachers with the professional 'tools' to provide their pupils with knowledge in a skilled way, resulting in long-term retention.

Professional learning: tight but loose

The tight but loose approach in the context of delivery of professional learning may be a useful notion for leaders. It's the idea that when we deliver training to teachers as leaders, we do so with the intention that the core and fundamental principles of what we deliver are secured and eventually embedded, with enough wiggle room for practioners to make these practices effective in the context of their classroom.

Adopting this approach does not necessarily reduce the effectiveness of the quality of implementation and may in fact improve the extent to which the intervention or approach is adopted in the classroom. As Dan Pink identified in his book *Drive* (2018), autonomy is a key component of human motivation and I would argue it needs to be considered in any implementation effort. Simply put, no one likes being told what to do with very little choice or sense of volition.

This, however, needs to be balanced with an unapologetic attention to the presence of the key ingredients of any implementation effort. The EEF refer to these key ingredients as 'active ingredients' and define these as 'a well specified set of "active ingredients" captures the essential principles and practices that underpin the approach. They are the key behaviours and content that make it work.'

Without this focus on the active ingredients, we lose our ability as leaders to optimise impactful implementation. The following diagram captures how this tight-loose approach may practically be achieved.

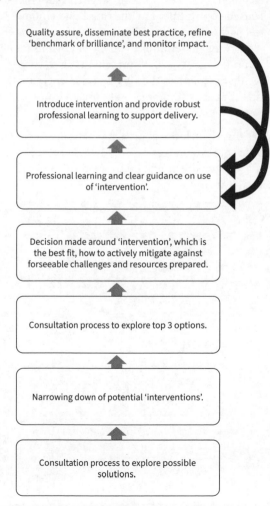

Quality assure, disseminate best practice, refine 'benchmark of brilliance', and monitor impact.

Introduce intervention and provide robust professional learning to support delivery.

Professional learning and clear guidance on use of 'intervention'.

Decision made around 'intervention', which is the best fit, how to actively mitigate against forseeable challenges and resources prepared.

Consultation process to explore top 3 options.

Narrowing down of potential 'interventions'.

Consultation process to explore possible solutions.

Figure 1: 'Tight but loose' in action

This diagram captures the different stages that a leader might engage with when implementing a new approach, which for the purposes of this visual I have referred to as an 'intervention', as referenced in the Education Endowment Foundation's guide to implementation (2019). The consultation process at the beginning allows teachers to be closely involved in the decision-making process organically from the very beginning of the process. This transparency and involvement in the exploration stage can support whole-hearted commitment to 'the cause' and empower staff to feel part of something. This sense of belonging can go a long way. In her book *Leading for Organisational Change*, Jennifer Emery (2019) presents a framework for change that recognises the very real challenges that accompany change within organisations and how these can be overcome.

What does this tight/loose approach practically look like in a real-life context? In this case study, Jade Pearce shares an example of how this might be adopted when delivering professional learning.

Jade Pearce

Case study: A tight but loose approach

I have found a tight but loose approach to leadership to be not only most effective but also vital. Being 'tight' means specifying those expectations that are common across the school. This enables us to create consistency where it matters most. Being 'loose' means trusting our teachers and giving them autonomy. It respects and utilises teacher expertise and is more likely to result in committed and motivated staff that are satisfied with their job and want to remain in our schools. While these approaches seem to be in contrast, it is possible to be tight on overarching approaches or principles, whilst being loose on how these are implemented.

Tight teaching and learning

In my school, we are passionate about evidence-informed pedagogy and its ability to help us to identify our 'best bets' – those strategies that are supported by research as being most likely to result in optimal teaching and learning, and so have the largest impact on pupil outcomes and life chances. Therefore, we are 'tight' when we expect all teachers to utilise these evidence-informed strategies.

To this end, evidence-informed T&L is the main priority of our school development plan. It is also included in all department development plans and all individual teachers' performance management targets. We also have a shared 'T&L Framework' that specifies the T&L principles we see as being most crucial in our school. This includes:

- Creating a positive classroom culture
- Explicit instruction
- Managing cognitive load
- Questioning and checking for understanding
- Challenge
- Literacy
- Retrieval practice and spacing
- Feedback

We utilised whole-school teaching and learning briefings to build a shared and consistent understanding of these strategies and ensure these approaches were embedded by all teachers. This included giving a clear explanation of each priority and the 'active ingredients' that are required to ensure the strategy is implemented most effectively, an exposition on the research and theory behind each new approach, and training on how to implement the strategies in the classroom.

We reinforce the need and ability of all teachers to use these strategies through revisiting them in further whole-school sessions, sharing best practice, reviewing each department's progress in embedding these strategies with heads of department regularly, and by focusing lesson drop-ins and any related feedback on these areas.

Loose teaching and learning

However, our T&L leadership is 'loose' in terms of how this is interpreted in classrooms. Firstly because we accept that each of the T&L strategies is likely to 'look' very different in different subjects. Retrieval practice should look different in English than it does in maths, or art and PE, as should modelling and feedback. Secondly, and linked to this, we trust our teachers as experts who can make decisions about their teaching and how initiatives can best be implemented in their disciplines.

To achieve this, after any whole-school session, we always give time for departments to discuss and decide how these strategies can be best implemented in their disciplines. This often takes place on Inset days so that departments have a prolonged period to focus on the strategies. This includes each department reading and discussing further research or articles about how the strategy has been successfully used in their subject and the opportunity to look at further subject-specific examples.

This also means that it is crucial for any T&L policy or framework to not be too specific or prescriptive. For instance, our framework states that retrieval practice should be used regularly, followed by corrective feedback, repeated over time and include both factual and higher order questions/tasks. However, it does not specify what format this should take or when retrieval practice should be completed by pupils.

Tight but loose professional development

In line with this, our professional development offer also has tight elements. All of the CPD opportunities available focus on our T&L framework and evidence-informed strategies. Our whole-school briefings discussed above are attended by all staff. However, we are also loose in this area, with individual CPD options. This aims to ensure that we take account of teachers' individual needs, areas of interest and level of expertise, and includes a range of options for teachers to choose from. This includes attending research sessions or pedagogy sessions or undertaking instructional coaching or independent reading. Furthermore, teachers can voluntarily undertake additional CPD including participating in our T&L Research Group, Pastoral Research Group, Curriculum Leaders Research Group, T&L Inquiry Group or external courses and qualifications such as the new suite of National Professional Qualifications.

Summary

A tight but loose approach can support school leaders in defining clear parameters for practice without stripping teachers of autonomy and creativity. It allows the 'best bets' from evidence-informed practice to guide how things are done, whilst still ensuring teachers maintain their professional judgement on *how* to achieve great outcomes for their pupils using these.

Reflective questions for your school

1. When might a tight but loose approach be useful in your school? When might it be less suitable?

2. How might I go about establishing a tight but loose approach to an intervention in my school?

3. What might be the potential issues around a tight but loose approach in my context?

References

Blase, K. A., Van Dyke, M., Fixsen, D. L. and Wallace Bailey, F. (2012). 'Implementation science: Key concepts, themes, and evidence for practitioners in educational psychology', in B. Kelly and D. F. Perkins, *Handbook of Implementation Science for Psychology in Education*. New York: Cambridge University Press, 13-66.

Education Endowment Foundation. (2019). Putting Evidence to Work: A school's guide to implementation, [Report], bit.ly/3ttej4w.

Emery, J. (2019). *Leading for Organisational Change: Building Purpose, Motivation and Belonging*. Chichester: Wiley.

Gelfand, M. (2018). *Rule makers, rule breakers: How tight and loose cultures wire our world*. New York: Simon & Schuster.

Gelfand, M. J., Raver, J. L., Nishii, L., Leslie, L. M., Lun, J., Lim, B. C., et al. (2011). 'Differences between tight and loose cultures: A 33-nation study', *Science*, 332(6033), 1100-1104.

Pink, D. (2018). *Drive: The Surprising Truth About What Motivates Us*. Edinburgh: Canongate Books.

Thompson, M. and Wiliam, D. (2008). Tight but Loose: A Conceptual Framework for Scaling Up School Reforms. Princeton, NJ: Educational Testing Service.

CHAPTERS

1	2	3	4	5	6	7	8	93
PAGE 15	PAGE 31	PAGE 45	PAGE 59	PAGE 69	PAGE 83	PAGE 95	PAGE 105	

CHAPTERS

| 1 | 2 | 3 | 4 | 5 | 6 | 7 | 8 | 95 |
| PAGE 15 | PAGE 31 | PAGE 45 | PAGE 59 | PAGE 69 | PAGE 83 | PAGE 95 | PAGE 105 | |

CHAPTER 7

A CULTURE OF CONTINUOUS IMPROVEMENT

| Chapter 7 | # A culture of continuous improvement |

Continuous improvement is the acceptance that the work is never done.

Hattie, 2014

'It really comes down to not who teachers are, not what they do, but how they think. And if they think primarily that their job is to evaluate their impact, all the good things follow.'

Continuous improvement implies that our professional knowledge and capacities aren't static. A culture of continuous improvement implies that we're ALL learning ALL of the time and therefore stamps out feelings of inadequacy, professional competition, and complacency.

The Japanese concept of *kaizen* (translates to 'good change') refers to the process of continuous improvement and is also a business philosophy, adopted widely in car manufacturing and other industries. This idea focuses on incremental change and can be usefully applied to the work of school improvement and cultivating the conditions to ensure high-quality outcomes and a sustained positive culture. In companies that adopt this culture, feedback is no doubt a routine part of what happens day to day. Quality circles are a way that this is achieved in some companies. This is where workers from different levels within an organisation come together to discuss problems and engage in collective problem-solving. In doing this, organisations can create a shared sense of ownership and promote a real sense of belonging. To 'get feedback right' is a crucial part of continuous improvement. How can conditions conducive of a culture of continuous improvement be achieved in schools and what are the key barriers to this as leaders?

In their book *Thanks for the Feedback: The Science and Art of Receiving Feedback Well*, Douglas Stone and Sheila Heen (2015) explore a very different take on feedback and how

CHAPTERS

1	2	3	4	5	6	7	8	97
PAGE 15	PAGE 31	PAGE 45	PAGE 59	PAGE 69	PAGE 83	**PAGE 95**	PAGE 105	

it could be considered. Rather than focusing on how to give feedback, they focus on how feedback is received by the recipient. The work in their book focuses on key ideas that could leverage the power of feedback-receiving and, therefore, optimise cultures of continuous improvement. This may be of particular use in addressing a key challenge of cultivating a culture of continuous improvement – feedback being perceived, accepted, and offered as developmental, *not* judgemental.

Stone and Heen define feedback as 'any time you get information about yourself'. In this vein, seeing your child's eyes light up when they see you sat in the audience at a recital is also considered feedback. They define three key barriers to receiving feedback:

1. Truth triggers: when we feel the feedback itself is inaccurate or unfair.
2. Relationship triggers: when the person giving you the feedback lacks credibility in your eyes, which in turn impacts the extent to which you 'buy' the feedback.
3. Identity triggers make us question who we are, leaving us feel threatened or ashamed.

The thing about this take on feedback is that it considers not only how to give feedback – an area that there is substantial guidance on both within and outside of education – but also how we can support the growth of a culture of accepting and acting upon feedback. By focusing attention on a culture that values and accepts feedback, we're able to pay deference to the fact that a) feedback is valuable and needs to be well-understood and b) that accepting feedback isn't always easy and that internalising and responding to feedback in a meaningful way requires a mindful approach.

A professional context does not diminish personal impact

One of the concepts that Stone and Heen refer to in the book is that of 'blind spots'. This fitting analogy recognises the gap between what we perceive about ourselves and what others perceive about us. This idea is best exemplified by the very common situation we often find ourselves in as humans, where

A culture of continuous improvement

our best intentions in a particular situation are not translated through our actions; the classic, 'I didn't mean for it to come across that way'. In our everyday interactions, this kind of misunderstanding is inevitable and hopefully does limited damage. When engaging in offering feedback, a process that is inherently personal and can lead to the emotional triggers mentioned above, it is even more important to be intentional about avoiding such emotional 'fallout'.

Stone and Heen suggest ways in which we can recognise our own blind spots and mitigate against these standing in the way of our own professional development. A few ways in which we can do this are:

- Recording ourselves and our practice as teachers to cut out the proverbial 'middleman' and see the feedback divorced entirely from the feedback-giver.
- Reflecting on ways in which we are 'standing in our own way' and even asking our feedback-givers the ways in which they perceive us doing this.
- Recognise your reaction to feedback and, rather than attributing the feedback to someone else's inaccurate judgements of you, consider whether the feedback is simply illuminating your 'blind spot'.

Now, of course, we can work on cultivating a culture where feedback is readily acceptable. But what can we do as leaders to support the acceptance of feedback (bar ensuring we do with these triggers in mind)? Stone and Heen highlight another pertinent point about feedback-givers that could support school leaders in instilling a culture of continuous improvement. What we think about the person giving us feedback undoubtedly impacts how we accept it. They draw attention to the three areas that influence acceptance of feedback from a given person:

1. Skill or professional judgement: we often disregard feedback from someone if we feel they lack the professional judgement to decide on the quality of our professional practice.
2. Trust: if we feel the person giving feedback isn't trustworthy and doesn't genuinely want to help us.

3. Credibility: if the person giving us feedback lacks credibility, e.g. if they haven't had enough experience within the domain, we are more likely to discredit their feedback.

These relationship triggers can offer school leaders an important insight into what might impact how our feedback 'lands'.

The idea of having knowledge that gives rise to 'credibility' also makes an appearance in Coe's (2022) research synthesis which cites Robinson et al's (2009) review where knowledge, skills and dispositions of leaders are broken down into four key dimensions:

1. Ensuring administrative decisions are informed by knowledge about effective pedagogy.
2. Analysing and solving complex problems.
3. Building relational trust.
4. Engaging in open-to-learning conversations.

Of note here are dimensions 1 and 4. Leaders need to have the domain-specific knowledge to be able to have the credibility that Stone and Heen mention. In addition to this, leaders (and teachers alike!) need to be able to engage in open-to-learning conversations. If leaders can model this and this skill can be disseminated within a school, the culture is more likely to be one that values and promotes continuous improvement.

In their 2022 report 'School Leadership Expertise', Tom Rees and Jennifer Barker of Ambition Institute highlight the importance of this domain-specific knowledge in school leadership. In the report, they define domain-specific expertise as the 'knowledge and skills with a specific field, domain or type of organisation'. They suggest that this deep knowledge is integral to impactful school leadership. In the foreword of this report, Viviane Robinson reminds us that the knowledge that leaders require to solve the complex problem of school improvement is not the same knowledge that an experienced classroom teacher would have acquired from years of experience in the classroom. It is therefore crucial for teachers to have a sound and

A culture of continuous improvement

deep understanding of behaviour and culture, pedagogy, assessment, and other school-specific domains.

Radical candour can support a culture of continuous improvement

Radical candour is the basis of a feedback framework, designed by Kim Scott, a nurse practioner from Princeton University. She defines 'radical candour' as being what happens at the crossroads of caring personally and challenging directly.

This means giving the feedback that is sometimes uncomfortable to give but will have major impact on the practice of those we lead.[1] In school cultures of continuous improvement, this radical candour is not only modelled by leaders and teachers alike, but also welcomed! As you might have guessed, this warrants a culture of psychological safety, as discussed earlier in the book, where it's ok to 'mess up'. When in receipt of candid feedback, we're accepting of its value, rather than being worried that we're being called out on something related to our practice.

Here, Heena Dave, curriculum designer at the Teacher Development Trust, explores how this domain specific knowledge shows up in the National Professional Qualifications and how these support school leaders in gaining this crucial knowledge.

1
Radical candour can still be delivered with compassion. Being candid doesn't equate to being cut-throat or harsh. Rather, it involves giving honest feedback from a place of care because you would rather that person not be in the dark about something that's potentially holding their practice back.

Heena Dave

Case study: Domain specific knowledge

How do NPQs equip leaders with domain specific knowledge? Why is it important for leaders to have this to solve problems?

In 2021 the reformed National Professional Qualifications (NPQ) were launched by the Department for Education. Within each of these qualifications the frameworks set out two types of content. This includes key evidence statements drawn from high-quality evidence alongside practical guidance on the skills school leaders should develop (DfE, 2021).

School leadership is complex. Achieving positive outcomes for all children and young people is dependent

CHAPTERS

1	2	3	4	5	6	7	8
PAGE 15	PAGE 31	PAGE 45	PAGE 59	PAGE 69	PAGE 83	**PAGE 95**	PAGE 105

101

on a school leader's expertise on school improvement, how professional environments are more likely to lead to improved teaching ability or understanding how pupils learn. In response to this breadth of interconnected knowledge, the newly reformed NPQ frameworks codify a series of evidence-informed domains and the associated knowledge that school leaders need to develop expert mental models.

It is only through being presented with such a comprehensive framework, explicitly containing core knowledge and skills, that school leaders can acknowledge and learn about the complexities of school leadership. For example, a school leader who has noticed that her pupils do not have high expectations for their own academic future may find it difficult to respond to such deep-seated beliefs without expert mental models developed through evidence-informed knowledge on behaviour, professional development, implementation, and school culture. From this perspective, the NPQ frameworks have been designed to help school leaders take a coherent and methodical approach to developing their own expertise across of a range of domains and in applying this expertise to the problems experienced within their own context.

Professional learning communities support continuous improvement

The concept of a professional learning community comes from the business sector and according to Vescio et al (2008) is grounded in two assumptions. Firstly, that its knowledge is situated in the lived experience of teachers and is best understood by reflecting on these with others who share the same experience (Buysse et al, 2003) and secondly that actively engaging in professional learning communities increases knowledge and subsequently enhances student learning.

In their review of 11 studies of the impact of professional learning communities on student learning and teaching practices, Vescio et al (2007) found that the collective results suggested that well-developed PLCs have a positive impact on both.

Vescio et al (2008) signposts the work of Newmann et al (1996) who describe professional learning communities as consisting of the given essential characteristics:

1. Shared values and norms must be developed.
2. A clear and consistent focus on student learning.
3. Reflective dialogue that leads to extensive conversation about curriculum instruction and student development.
4. De-privatising practice to make teaching public.
5. A focus on collaboration.

Although many of the 11 studies didn't describe a specific change to pedagogy, it did describe that PLCs significantly contributed to the shift in the 'habits of mind that teachers bring to their daily work in the classroom'.

Summary

A culture of continuous improvement in schools means that conversations around improvement are frequent, regular, and warmly welcomed. Rather than the focus being on teachers' emotional triggers around receiving the feedback, the focus shifts to the feedback itself, thus enabling quicker gains in quality of delivery on the ground. This is something that we can model as leaders by 'always learning' ourselves but also instil in our schools with a continuous focus on 'doing better'.

Reflective questions for your school

1. What are the attitudes towards coaching and feedback in my school?
2. How can I support a culture of continuous improvement practically?
3. What contextually might be a barrier for sustaining a culture of continuous improvement?

References

Barker, J. and Rees, T. (2022). 'School Leadership Expertise', Ambition Institute.

Buysse, V., Sparkman, K. L. and Wesley, P. W. (2003). 'Communities of Practice: Connecting What We Know with What We Do', *Exceptional Children*, 69(3).

Coe, R. (2022). 'School Environment and Leadership: Evidence Review', Evidence Based Education.

Hattie, J. (2014, August 25). *The Educators: John Hattie* [Radio interview]. BBC Radio 4. bbc.co.uk/programmes/b04dmxwl.

Newmann, F. M., Marks, H. M. and Gamoran, A. (1996). 'Authentic Pedagogy and Student Performance', *American Journal of Education*, 104(4), 280-312.

Stone, D. and Heen, S. (2015). *Thanks for the feedback*. Portfolio Penguin.

Vescio, V. A., Ross, D. D. and Adams, A. (2008). 'A review of research on the impact of professional learning communities on teaching practice and student learning', *Teaching and Teacher Education*, 24, 80-91.

| Chapter 8 | **Collective wisdom** |

CHAPTERS

1	2	3	4	5	6	7	8
PAGE 15	PAGE 31	PAGE 45	PAGE 59	PAGE 69	PAGE 83	PAGE 95	**PAGE 105**

105

CHAPTER 8

COLLECTIVE WISDOM

| Chapter 8 | **Collective wisdom** |

Craft expertise from leaders in the field.

This book offers a whistle-stop tour of how leaning into our most human tendencies can enhance school culture and in turn improve outcomes for pupils. I don't claim to be an expert in the field but if there's one thing I'm sure of from my years of experience, it's that school culture matters.

I'm forever grateful to colleagues who challenge my ideas and thinking, as they genuinely strengthen my understanding and knowledge at every turn. In this brief closing chapter, I defer to the wisdom of colleagues in the sector who have lived and breathed school culture. I close by presenting a model of professional learning for leaders that includes some of the key components of culture I have presented throughout the book, in the hope that it raises further awareness of the importance of school culture.

How can we build strong school culture?

Rachel Higginson, educational consultant

'…*by being relentlessly conscious and proactively present. You cannot support growth without constantly understanding where your people are "at". All staff, pupils and community… You also cannot grow a culture from behind a closed door… conscious and present…*'

Liz Russo Easaw, director of primary education

'*It's all about strong relationships and integrity. Children know and experience that they are loved through nurture, boundaries and challenge. Doing this builds trust with families and staff when we follow through and our policies match our actions and decisions.*'

Jade Pearce, assistant head

'*For me, culture is the values and beliefs of a school in action. It's what we value and see as most important. And it determines our priorities, our leadership, what it feels like to work at the school. Cracking culture takes time. Your actions, decisions and communication have to demonstrate your values. You have to show (through real actions, continuously) that you value and trust staff, value PD, value academic and wider success equally.*'

'Cracking school culture is all about nurturing small, common and positive behaviours.'

'Culture is grown and nurtured. It's a distillation of many bothered voices. It doesn't happen in a single act, it's a common act of all being on the same page believing in the direction and pushing together. True culture has many hours of listening before doing.'

David Nautilus, headteacher

Simon Smith, principal

References

Coe, R., Kime, S., and Singleton, D. (2022). School Environment and Leadership: Evidence Review, A model for school environment and leadership, *Evidence Based Education*, bit.ly/3E2siDb.

Appendix

APPENDIX

Here, I offer a potential framework that could be used to support leaders in developing their understanding encompassing the different facets of school culture explored throughout this book. This is intended to supplement the domain-specific core knowledge required by leaders to effectively impact change in their educational settings. This is by no means the finished article but is a potential avenue by which leaders could be supported in tying together these components of culture with the practical elements required for school improvement.

	Module	Strand 1 - Purpose and Vision	Strand 2 - Culture and Collaboration		Strand 3 - Evaluation and Reflection	Strand 4 - Rethinking and Refining	
Core Text and Literature	Module 1	Start with Why, Simon Sinek / Thanks for the Feedback, Douglas Stone, Sheila Heen	Conversations for Action, Fernando Flores	Radical Candor, Kim Scott / The Fearless Organisation, Amy Edmondson	Drive, Dan Pink	Think Again: The Power of Knowing What You Don't Know, Adam Grant	Connect, Simon Lancaster
Intent	Module 1	'Start with Why' – purpose and context	School Environment and Leadership 'What makes a difference?' Evidence Base in Education- Shared vision	Aligning your purpose and practice for instructional leadership (Harvard Graduate School of Education) – Revisiting purpose	Evaluating progress against intent – a collaborative process	Adam Grant – Rethinking	Reinforcing and recommunicating your why – purpose
	Module 2	Subject audit and action planning – now, next, then	Conversations for possibility – Fernando Flores	Radical Candor – Kim Scott	Dan Pink – long-term motivation – motivating others to understand and engage in your vision	What makes a difference? – Distributed leadership	ACTION RESEARCH SHARE

Implementation	Module 3	EEF's Implementation Guide	What makes a difference? – Cultivating leadership trust	Amy Edmondson – Psychological safety	Ensuring fidelity and support mechanisms	Supporting struggling teachers with implementation	Annual review of implementation – a collaborative process
	Module 4	Designing impactful professional learning / Communicating with clarity	What makes a difference? – Support for effective professional development	Psychological safety in professional learning	Designing impactful professional learning	Preparing for reset and restart- designing Inset professional learning	Preparing for reset and restart – designing Inset professional learning
Impact	Module 5	What does it mean to have impact? – quality assurance and monitoring	Quality assurance and monitoring for school improvement	Analysis pupil's learning – HGSE	Exemplifying excellence – benchmarks of brilliance	Codifying excellence for new staff	Reporting on impact and course correction
	Module 6	'Thanks for the Feedback' – how to deliver feedback to effect sustained change	Quality assurance and monitoring for school improvement – reporting and course correction	'Thanks for the feedback' – how to deliver feedback to effect sustained change	360 feedback and self-reflection	'Thanks for the feedback' – how to deliver feedback to effect sustained change	Self-reflection as a leader